FASHION TEXTILES NOW

FASHION TEXTILES NOW

Janet Prescott

VIVAYS PUBLISHING

Published by Vivays Publishing Ltd
www.vivays-publishing.com

© 2013 Janet Prescott

A catalogue record for this book is available from the
British Library

ISBN 978-1-908126-35-1

Publishing Director: Lee Ripley
Designer: Raymonde Watkins

Cover: Courtesy Schoeller®, Switzerland
Frontispiece: Courtesy Chanel Press Office

Printed in China

Contents

Introduction   page 8

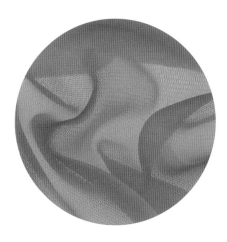

1
Animal fibres

page 10

2
Plant fibres

page 58

3
**Synthetic
and high-tech
fabrics**

page 90

Picture credits   page 174
Index   page 175

4

Eco fabrics and sustainability

page 106

5

Heritage fabrics

page 124

6

Fabric to fashion

page 154

Introduction

FASHION is high profile, a sexy subject that sells magazines, TV programmes and newspapers. Fashion blogs are the most popular genres on the net and exclusive designer shows, live-streamed from Fashion Week catwalks around the world, invite us to be in the front row and imagine we're all celebrities.

We are all experts in fashion, but how much are we told about the most important element, the place where fashion starts — the fabric. How much do you know about fabrics? And does it matter?

Actually, it matters a lot – no matter what price level you are looking at. The fact is you can have the best-designed garment in the world, but unless the fabric is right, it won't last, feel good or look right.

The textile industry is active all over the globe. Behind what you see on the catwalks, there is a whole hidden system that combines industry, glamour, high finance and above all, design. Its scope ranges from high-tech industrial manufacturing to traditional spinning and weaving. It encompasses haute couture and tailoring for the elite to handmade fabrics made on traditional looms and the everyday clothing we buy in our favourite shops. It is leading the heritage revival, driving the renaissance of old established mills and skills, and playing a part in the growing focus on sustainability and ecologically sound manufacture.

The industry's constant appetite for raw materials is fed by huge flocks of animals reared for their fleeces in the southern hemisphere, and vast crops of cotton, flax and hemp. The age-old skills of knitting and weaving are being nurtured by designers in Japan, Italy and France. At the same time, large business conglomerates are investing in textiles, planting bamboo and beech forests and conducting high-tech scientific research into new fibres in South Korea, Germany and Austria. Fashion names like LVMH in France, Marks and Spencer in the UK, Ralph Lauren or Tommy Hilfiger in the US, Isetan in Japan are watched as indicators of global economic health.

In fact, fabrics are a strange mixture of big business, love, craft, art and creativity. The textile industry is one of the most international and complex trades, with the raw materials and manufacture of textiles and clothing carried on in inter-dependent economies all over the world. It has led to the development of huge manufacturing capabilities in China and India as well as fuelling expanding economies like Brazil and Russia. Yet at the same time, it is responding to the intense pressure applied by groups seeking to improve working conditions and abolish the exploitation of the workforce that is still a problem in some parts of the world, as well as the need to reduce damaging pollution.

The fabric trade is largely anonymous and not understood by most people. Its star designers, who have high artistic reputations within the industry, are almost unknown except to those professionals. Few people can name a fabric brand except perhaps Liberty, Tencel, Harris Tweed, Lurex, Goretex or the elastic fibre Lycra.

Yet the trade has an influence on how we live. Textiles virtually kick-started the green movement and sustainable manufacturing, after being responsible for a large part of the pollution produced in industrial areas in the past. It can use everything from a hill of beans to real diamonds or wild nettles to make into clothes you want to wear. It also produces millions of metres of polyester and cotton per year.

So how much do you know about what you're wearing? Have a go at this to test your knowledge:

What's viscose?

Can you wear milk and coffee?

Is your underwear made of crab shells?

*Which luxury suiting was worn by mods and punks and also
international bankers?*

Can you ever wear your suit in the shower?

What's special about Harris Tweed?

Which creatures produce silk apart from silkworms?

*How can worn-out jeans be resurrected for a second life?
What does recycled polyester start life as?*

*What does an alpaca look like, a merino sheep, or a vicuna, angora
or cashmere goat? And which has the Bambi factor?*

How can your clothes protect you from harm?

What's a micro-climate?

*And what's the single most important thing you can do when buying
clothes to help you recognise high quality, to make the most of your money,
or to follow your desire to help save the planet?*

If you didn't know all the answers, this book will fill in some of the gaps.

1
Animal fibres

Animal fibres

Can you ever wear your suit in the shower?

There is now a wool fabric that you can shower overnight, even while you wear it, and it will be perfectly dry in the morning.

Fabrics made from animal fibres are perhaps the most well known of all, especially in the more northern countries. The main fibres collected from animals which we know about in fashion and clothing are wool, cashmere, mohair, alpaca, and scarce precious speciality fibres such as vicuña and Cervelt™, a newly developed natural fibre from hair combed from the under-down of the New Zealand red deer. Wool is the best known and most widely used of these, and the majority comes from Merino sheep that are raised in Australia New Zealand, South Africa and South America. Speciality heritage wool breeds are also increasingly used in fashion.

WOOL

PEOPLE think they know about wool. It brings to mind jumpers as comfortable as the knits worn by Wallace in *Wallace and Grommit*, the thick hardwearing fisherman's Guernsey sweater you take on holiday, and the venerable tweed jacket worn by everyone's dad. But there's a lot more to it than that.

Wool has come a long way from the scratchy, heavy knit stockings and vest materials older generations remember. Today's wool is a comfort fibre, light and soft. It can be as sophisticated as the flowing, featherweight knits dreamed up by top designers, or the hip highly patterned chunky sweaters worn in cult Scandinavian detective TV series. It is knitted into warm jackets and dresses or fine lacy fashion or sporty casuals.

Wool is the main component of the most sophisticated suits in the world. Wool yarn, twisted or combed is woven into luxury outfits, whether from Savile Row, Giorgio Armani or the High Street boutique, making exquisitely light and sophisticated cloth to make perfect suits worn by world leaders, royalty and military top brass. Uncreasable suits with Lycra and traditional green loden and Crombie overcoats can be seen worn by smart travellers of every nationality in every airport in the world. Pure wool is sometimes blended with cashmere, angora, or alpaca for extra luxury fabrics, or has precious stones spun into the mix such as diamonds, jade or gold thread.

The more wool in a garment, the better it will feel and it's enjoying a resurgence because it has street-cred for retro looks and it's also a star of the fashion shows, with major designers using the best quality wool fabrics from Britain and Italy for edgy urban wear.

Wool and animal fibres

Wool is by far the most important of the animal fibres, worn almost everywhere, in every climate, including in hot environments. You'll notice a much greater percentage of wool in new winter clothing. Blends of wool and synthetics such as polyester are featuring more wool, as the advantages of the natural fibre are recognised and the movement towards sustainable living grows.

Hainsworth coat – history meets fashion

Savile Row reports that younger clients are increasingly coming to the famous names of Savile Row like Anderson and Sheppard, Richard James, Ozwald Boateng, Gieves and Hawkes, Henry Poole, Hardy Amies, Huntsman as soon as they can afford it. The appeal of garments tailor-made from top quality fabrics for individuals keeps its allure. It's a long tradition built over centuries.

Uniforms for state occasions have been woven for over two hundred years by British mills, particularly A W Hainsworth in Yorkshire, a seven-generation family firm. Princes William and Harry, as well as the two pageboys, were dressed in uniforms made from the cloth at the royal wedding in 2011. This striking red coat is fashioned out of traditional red military cloth woven in Yorkshire, by Hainsworth, as it has been for over a century. It caused quite a stir in the press when it was first unveiled on the catwalk, designed by Anita Massarella.

Merino flock in Australia

Did you know that Merino sheep are 'grown'? This is the word the professionals use for the production of vast numbers of sheep and prodigious amounts of the finest wool in Southern Australia. Huge ranches rear millions of sheep which are selected for their copious wool. Merino wool is fine, soft and luxurious and is known for its soft touch, and also for its built-in advantages in keeping the wearer warm in winter and cool in summer. Merino can be substantial and thick but also fine and gauzy, depending on the thickness of the spun yarn and gauge, or thickness, of the needles it is knitted on and how it's woven.

Merino flock at dawn

The raising and shearing of sheep is a massive undertaking in Australia, South America, the USA and South Africa, the principal areas where sheep are reared for their fleece. In Australia this important part of the wool year has led to the figure of the travelling sheep shearer and inspired many folk songs and stories, including Australia's unofficial anthem, *Waltzing Matilda*. Sheep, wool and all that goes with it seem wired into the DNA of the country. This romantic view of sheep in the sunshine fits the image. Wool represents about 2 per cent of world fibre production, but punches above its weight in terms of desirability, availability and looking good.

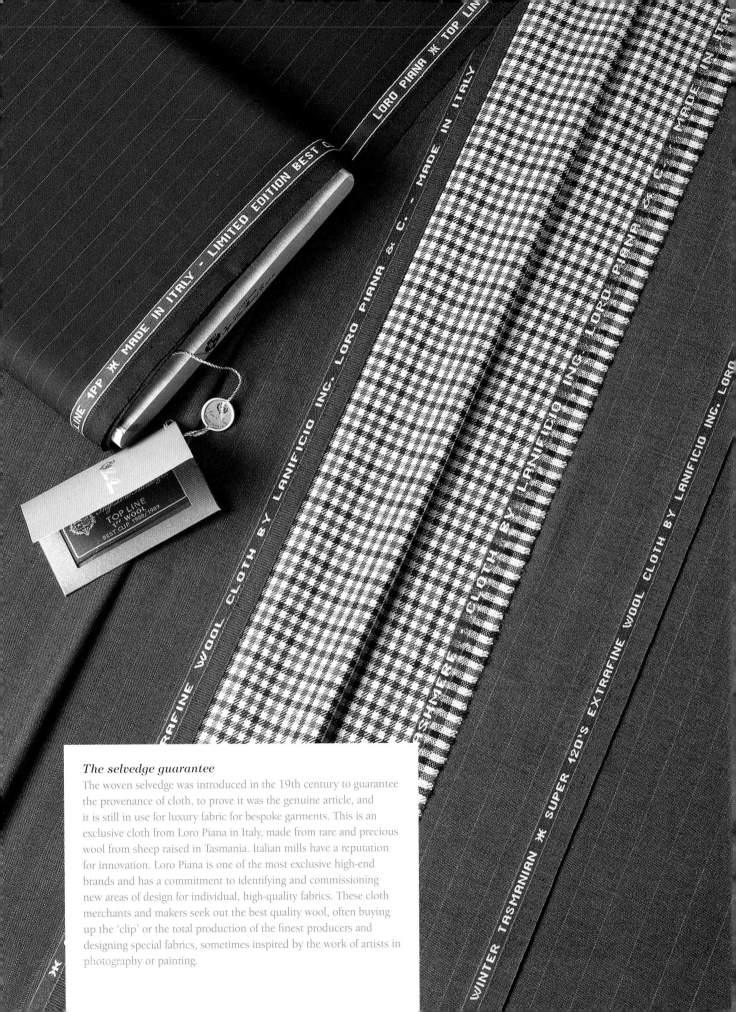

The selvedge guarantee

The woven selvedge was introduced in the 19th century to guarantee
the provenance of cloth, to prove it was the genuine article, and
it is still in use for luxury fabric for bespoke garments. This is an
exclusive cloth from Loro Piana in Italy, made from rare and precious
wool from sheep raised in Tasmania. Italian mills have a reputation
for innovation. Loro Piana is one of the most exclusive high-end
brands and has a commitment to identifying and commissioning
new areas of design for individual, high-quality fabrics. These cloth
merchants and makers seek out the best quality wool, often buying
up the 'clip' or the total production of the finest producers and
designing special fabrics, sometimes inspired by the work of artists in
photography or painting.

There is more wool fabric around for both summer and winter these days. Just look at the labels in the clothes you're thinking of buying. However, while a mix with large amounts of polyester might make for a cheaper garment, the feel and comfort of the fabric will be compromised.

Wool is also the ultimate heritage fibre. The extravagant, prolific fleeces of the wonderful Merino sheep and the centuries old pure Escorial breed of sheep, prized for its crimped fibre and soft, lustrous handle, were both reared for the princes of Europe, and moved across the continent of Europe to Australia and New Zealand where they flourished. There are still more sheep than people in New Zealand. Australia is the powerhouse of promoting wool. In the UK the Prince of Wales inaugurated the Campaign for Wool that is bringing wool back into the spotlight internationally, making headlines with flocks of sheep brought to London, New York and Paris and promoting the wool creations of designers like Vivienne Westwood.

Wool is connected with the British Isles and the names prove it. Shetland, Herdwick, Cheviot, Harris tweed, Guernseys, Jerseys and Fair Isle are all wool terms showing the origin of the native hardy British sheep and places they originated from; ranging from offshore islands in the north of Scotland to the pastures of the west of England, woven or knitted into traditional patterns which are very fashionable.

Knitted into warm jackets and dresses or fine lacy fashion or sporty casuals, sports wool has also kitted out football teams and the Aussie cricketers. In iconic designs like the bright Scottish tartans or soft grey flannel, it's made into skirts, kilts, jackets and suits. Patterns such as the Prince of Wales check, herringbones, houndstooth checks, birds-eyes and windowpanes all describe retro designs that are still in vogue.

You might not know that wool is also a techno-fibre with strong ecological credentials; it has natural anti-UV properties for protection from the sun, is naturally flame retardant and water resistant. As a fibre that is closely related to the structure of human skin, it reacts to heat and cold to keep you comfortable. Sheep run free and their wool is biodegradable and renewable. *Cool Wool*, a concept recently relaunched by Woolmark (one of the most recognised logos in the world), is an ultra-lightweight fabric made from fine, soft Merino wool fibre that can be worn in comfort during the summer.

The boon of washable wool is expected by most consumers, but now wool suits have been developed that can be washed in a normal washing machine, and even hung up to dry overnight after being washed in the shower! But don't try this with your bespoke pure wool tailor-made version. Read the label first!

Sheep Breeds

British wool is usually thought of as the wool of the quintessential woolly jumper and knitted tank top. The sometimes extraordinary looking sheep are ancient breeds with thicker, coarser wool than the Merino, but with remarkable thermal properties. The wool has kept Northern people warm over generations, including fishermen, hillwalkers and workers, and it has been used in the traditional patterns which are regularly used in fashion collections.

Some of these sheep, like Jacobs or Shetlands, have given their names to particular designs and cloths, mostly used in country wear or smart/casual urban designs. The Fair Isles, Shetlands and Harris are all islands off the coast of Scotland, Jersey and Guernsey are in the English Channel, all have given their names to iconic jumpers. Cheviot cloth is a country weave associated with the wool of sheep reared on the Cheviot Hills on the Scottish/English border. Donegals are wonderful speckled tweeds and knits from Donegal in Ireland.

Wool spun on the worsted system, involving only longer, parallel fibres, gives a finer, smoother cloth. The luxury end of the market is particularly associated with Savile Row, the famous London street where the bespoke tailors have traditionally clothed the international movers and shakers of the past two hundred years.

If you walk along Savile Row now, some basements can still be seen from the road, where the tailors cut, sew and fashion the cloth into garments fitted exactly to the measurements of individual clients. It is a must for the visitor to London.

Clockwise from top left: *Wensleydale, Jacob, Southdown and Blueface*

Merino sheep

Merino sheep have been compared to judges in full wigs, the curly fleece framing their long nosed faces with a magnificent gravity. These are New Zealand Merinos in full pomp. New Zealand Merino has created a brand standard called Zque that means the sheep have been raised in a responsible and sustainable manner, are of the highest quality and can be traced to individual farms. Provenance or traceability is a growing trend throughout the textile industry, providing a guarantee of quality and origin for the end user who is concerned about where their clothing originates, and the quality of all the stages it goes through.

Vivienne Westwood Gold collection in Australian Merino wool

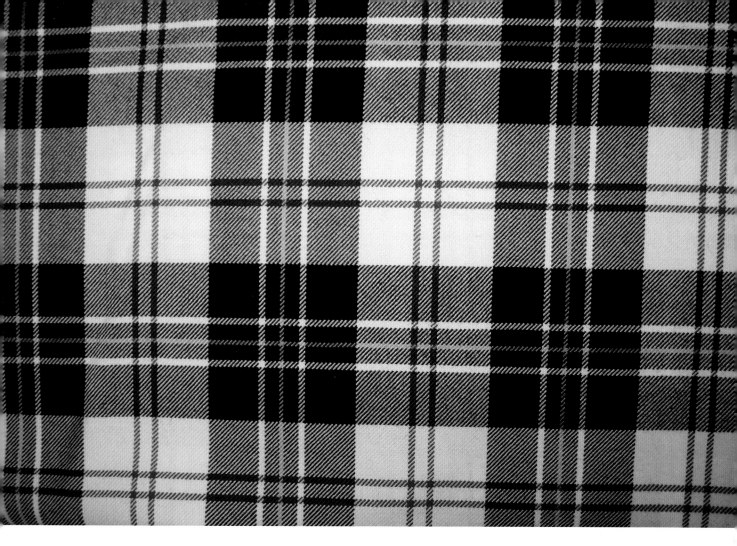

MacPherson dress tartan in wool from Lochcarron of Scotland

Pre-spun wool

This is a picture of wool pre-spinning showing its volume and fluffiness. Extra fine wool with very little weight and an airy volume is used for knitwear that is lightweight as well as soft to the touch. Even thicker fabrics are now much lighter and can be used by designers for knitwear that looks as chunky as the traditional designs. Today lighter weights are preferred, used in layers for a very versatile look that can be adapted for all different temperatures.

Many wool garments can be cleaned in a washing machine, but the advice is to always read the label. Wool clothes do not need to be ironed. The fibre can naturally regulate the body's temperature and provide protection against the elements including rain, heat, cold and harmful rays from the sun (UV). Treatments such as Teflon can make wool fabrics stain resistant.

Escorial rams

Escorial sheep are an ancient breed whose history symbolises the history of Western Europe. Bred for their light, soft wool, in the 17th century the sheep were owned by King Philip II of Spain and were jealously guarded as valuable possessions. In 1765 some of the flock were presented to the Elector of Saxony, present day Germany, where the soft handle fabrics created from the fleece were called Saxonies, a fabric type that is still recognised. In 1850 an enterprising Scotswoman took 100 sheep with her when she emigrated to Australia, and successfully raised them. Although in Europe the Escorial and Saxony flocks died out, three flocks now remain in Australia with a pure bloodline and their descendants are reared in both Australia and New Zealand.

Escorial sheep produce a helix shaped crimped fibre that can be woven into sumptuous yet light garments. The yarn created from this rare wool is woven into fabric by exclusive mills in Yorkshire and Italy. Suits made of Escorial wool usually bear the label.

Powerful elegance

It's no coincidence that men in powerful positions are sometimes called 'suits'. The suit is probably the most potent symbol of authority, worn formally with a shirt and tie and as a mark of a new style of power, worn with an open-necked shirt. The acme of suits is the made-to-measure, bespoke version where clever measuring, cutting and sewing result in a suit that fits the wearer perfectly.

Archives from Savile Row yield up fascinating details of changing tastes, personal proclivities and the way society has changed. The traditional clientele was formerly made up generations of the aristocracy, then included business leaders in the 20th century and now in the 21st attracts celebrities, from musicians to film stars, politicos and financiers on a global scale. Many people in the Middle East wear both Western designed suits by well-known designers and also wear dishdash robes in fine worsted wool often woven by specialists such as Taylor and Lodge in Huddersfield, Yorkshire, or Scabal who have their own mill in the Pennines.

The mystique of 'The Row', as Savile Row is commonly called, is carefully managed. The image of luxurious elegance can be summed up by this picture of an immaculately clad man wearing luxury Scabal worsted fabric pictured with a correspondingly elegant horse.

Transparently delicate wool

This image shows how light and delicate garments from Merino wool can be. It can drape beautifully and be almost transparent. Australian Merino sheep produce very fine wool, measured in microns (1 micron=1/25,400in), which indicate the diameter of the fibre. The finest wool fibre may measure less than 18 microns, and would be spun into the most delicate yarns which might be used to make diaphanous fabrics for delicate dresses, skirts, and even ball gowns and wedding dresses. Who would have thought that wool could be such a seductive and sensuous medium? Merino is also used for comfortable next to skin antistatic and moisture-regulating bodywear.

Diamonds on the sleeve of your suit

Even more recherché is the fashion for including precious stones in the weave of the suit. This is Scabal's diamond chip fabric. There are also gold threads, silver and lapis lazuli that can be carefully incorporated in the yarn to give it sheen, a bit of glitter and flashes of colour. The subtlety of the cloth is part of its attraction; the jewel fragments are only visible when seen close up, but knowing that you're wearing diamonds on the sleeves of your suit gives a feeling of exclusivity and value that is much prized, particularly by Russian clients, it is said.

Today's fashion icon: new in 1805

Some garments are so famous that they have acquired their own names, the Macintosh, the Barbour jacket, and wool overcoats like the British Warm, and the Crombie named after the company which made it.

Crombie have now brought out a highly fashionable retro version of the classic Crombie, an elegant single-breasted woollen coat in dark navy usually with a satin lining. Many of the styles produced by the most serious and elegant companies have a touch of the dandy about them: the striped suit, accompanied by patterned silk handkerchief, bright silk tie and shirt. Jackets often have surprising linings with bright purple, red or pink satin. This image of the wool Crombie sums up all these elements.

All that glisters is fashion

Other precious stones and metals used by luxury producers are jade and lapis lazuli. Gold, silver and copper can also be incorporated into fabric, giving an expensive, sophisticated glitter. In addition, silver is used in fabrics for its anti-bacterial properties. Dormeuil 's jade cloth has a hint of the green stone visible in its wool worsted fabric, while Italian spinner Filpucci has produced beautiful metallic yarns with copper, bronze and silver as seen above.

Italian elegance – a driver of fashion

Many people ask what professionals do when they attend fabric shows, which happen twice yearly. Thousands of designers and buyers flock to Milan, Paris, Florence, and Munich to view and select yarns, fabrics and colours to use as the basis for their collections in summer and winter of the following year. The international buyers range from top couture names, to famous brands and designer labels to the buyers for the High Street. The process involves sampling, designing and ordering raw materials, dyestuffs and transport months in advance, with the production carefully staged to fit the manufacturing process and customer requirements. Millions of pounds and dollars, and many people's jobs worldwide are at stake.

These fabrics, by famous Italian weaving companies Reda and Angelico, show a lightweight fashionable wool which is called Frescodilana and a micro design by Angelico. They were shown at Idea Biella in Milan to buyers from markets such as Japan, Russia, the US and Europe. The designs will lead the trends for each season which will be worn from New York to New Delhi.

Le grand luxe – essential elements

Luxury fabrics demand luxury presentation. This bright blue box echoes the stratospheric colours of luxury worsted fabric Matterhorn Blue, produced by elite Anglo-French wool merchants Dormeuil, who weave their own fabric in Yorkshire. Matterhorn Blue was designed to mark the 170th anniversary of Dormeuil, based in Paris, which was founded in 1842.

Luxury fabric makers sell their fabric all around the world to the most exclusive outlets and in their own stores. They are expanding in Europe and the Far East, including China, producing both the finest quality fabrics and a constant fund of innovative designs.

The young ones – fashion talent rewarded

It's interesting that fabric design is attracting talents like Harriet Toogood
who, in 2011 was a winner at the prestigious annual Texprint award for young
designers in the UK. The work of the finalists is displayed in the designer section
of Indigo + Premiere Vision, the international fabric exhibition in Paris, where
the prizes have been presented by top designers such as Zandra Rhodes, Alber
Elbaz, Paul Smith and agnès b. Texprint and its industry supporters provide an
invaluable opportunity for young designers to network and show their work in
an international arena, and the winners go on to exhibit in Spinexpo, Shanghai.
Harriet won the Woolmark prize at Texprint 2011 with this design, which
combines the appeal of wool with inspired colour mastery and technical ability.

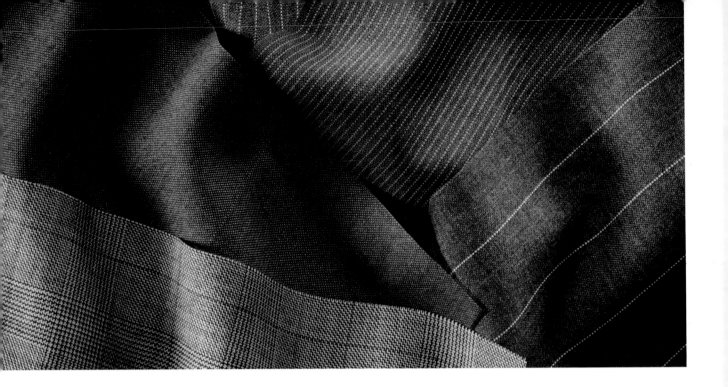

Look at the label!

There is a lot more information given on the labels inside clothes these days as stores realise that customers are interested in where their clothes come from, their provenance. Alfred Brown, long-established Yorkshire manufacturers of trendy woollen fabrics with a heritage twist, feature updated classics that are often inspired by their archives. Their fabric label has appeared on several ranges carried by big stores in the UK. As consumers demand a greater knowledge of what they are wearing, this trend looks to continue.

Knit style – it's all in the pattern

Patterned knitwear, based on traditional designs with a highly decorated yoke in contrasting colours, has been inspired by vintage patterns that include the classic Scottish geometric and flower-based designs. Usually interpreted in thicker gauge, chunky wools, they are surprisingly lightweight and soft to wear, which has made them more appealing to people who are more likely to drive a car or take public transport rather walking. Though the fact that more people are cycling to work and pursuing active outdoor activities is also leading to a revival of heavier fabrics worked in a traditional way. This fashionable patterned sweater is by John Smedley.

Knitwear twice as fashionable now

Knitwear is more versatile than weave and lately it has been in the forefront of fashion. It is easier and quicker to knit than to set up a loom for weaving and modern computer controlled machinery has ensured that knitting can be done at tremendous speed with perfect accuracy. Wool knitwear is newly popular, mainly because it has lost the image of scratchiness which it had in the past. The versatility of knitwear as a medium means it can be high tech for active sportswear, romantic for floaty designs and ruggedly masculine in vintage style. It is also at the vanguard of the handcraft revival. John Smedley, based in Leicestershire in England is one of the famous names in wool knitwear and is considered highly fashionable. Most high-quality wool garments will last for years and though often based on timeless designs, have a fashionable edge.

Knitwear tells a tale

Luxury knitwear in classic designs with a twist uses unusual high-quality materials like organic wool and wool from specific breeds of sheep, such as Geelong and Merino. Alan Paine is one of the famous long-established names in luxury British knitwear, using wool and lambswool as its principal materials. The company has a history dating from 1907 and rapidly became popular with the elite of the day. The Duke of Windsor was pictured wearing Alan Paine Argyle patterned (diamond pattern) sweaters. Famously, there is a connection to pioneering mountaineer George Mallory who went missing when climbing Everest on one of the first expeditions in 1924. His body was found on Everest in 1999. He was identified from the Mallory nametag, which was sewn next to the label *WF Paine, Godalming*, 75 years earlier.

This Alan Paine design is in chunky wool, from the Explorer collection.

LEFT *Tartan's not just for kilts*
OPPOSITE *Playing with checks*

Many younger tailors and designers in Savile Row also lend their talents to ready-to-wear fashion. Timothy Everest is one such tailor who is engaging with different areas, designing for brands such as Superdry, as well as designing his own line of bespoke clothing. Everest's designs are often outfits with a difference, like Everest's Glen check jacket and checked three-piece suit, worn by actor Noah Huntley.

The importance of finishing

Finishing is the method which changes and refines the appearance of a woven cloth. This John Foster suit is made from fine-quality 150s pure wool cloth by Luxury Fibres, famous for wool, mohair and precious blends, in 150s pure wool, a very fine quality. It is an example of the more casual approach which younger people are taking to, wearing a two or three-piece suit. The suit may be very luxurious and top of the range, but it can be dressed down or up according to mood. Finishers treat the cloth after weaving and make it shiny, matt, shrunk or stretched, carrying out one of the most important parts of the manufacturing process. Some of these finishes have acquired special names like the 'London Shrunk' here by WT Johnson of Yorkshire.

ABOVE *Sheep in The Row*
LEFT ***Exmoor sheep in Savile Row for Campaign for Wool***

The sight of sheep roaming along Savile Row in central London, with tweed-clad farmers and perky sheepdogs, was not some idyllic scene from a film set in the middle ages, but a real-life event staged in 2010. The event was repeated in many capitals, including Paris in 2012 with more planned in the coming years. This was the result of the Campaign for Wool, initiated in October 2008 by His Royal Highness the Prince of Wales in response to the challenges facing the wool industry, particularly from synthetic fibres.

Wool is one of the most environmentally friendly and sustainable of fibres. "At a time when concerns about landfills occupy us all, why on earth were we turning our backs on wool?" asked Prince Charles. The Campaign for Wool is already proving very effective in raising wool's profile worldwide. It is multinational, multi-sector and inclusive, for wool users from the largest companies to specialist artisans. Watch out for more flocks in a city near you in the future, and for the green sheep logo in shop displays and clothing labels.

FACT

There is enough wool on the average adult sheep to make
3 men's suits,
6 dresses,
or 70 pairs of socks.

CASHMERE AND PRECIOUS FIBRES
Alpaca, Camel hair, Vicuña, Cervelt

Cashmere

Cashmere is the best known of the precious fibres and it's still a special purchase, ranking along with champagne, fine wines and pearls as an item to appreciate. It comes from the coats of nimble wild goats reared in Asia: Mongolia, China, India, Iran and the 'Stans' which include Kyrgyzstan, Afghanistan and Pakistan where the goats live in the high cold mountains and develop soft, insulating hair to keep them warm. This hair is then combed from the animals and the fibres are transformed into yarn for knitwear and woven fabrics.

Cashmere is generally used in rather expensive, beautiful knitwear and high-quality cashmere is hard to beat for softness and luxury. It is also employed in luxury woven fabric for top quality suits, jackets and tailored clothing. At first it was difficult to mix with other fibres but now spinners have found a way to blend it with wool, silk and other yarns such as linen so you'll see it more often in a wide range of shops.

Although it is mainly known for its exquisite colours, in its natural state cashmere fibre ranges in colour from white to grey and brown. The fibre takes colour well and can be dyed into bright shades, jewel tones and equally successfully into heathery, subtle country tones which are very difficult to translate into other fibres.

Recently, the higher prices for cashmere have actually cheered cashmere spinners, weavers and knitters. They were beginning to be seriously troubled by the effect of mass-market cashmere knits made from shorter, inferior fibres that were being sold at one stage into many supermarkets and lower quality brands. Often these inferior fibres neither performed as well nor lasted as long as traditional knitwear and the trade suspected this was beginning to damage the fibre's image.

Scottish cashmere has an international reputation. The yarn spun there is of extremely high quality and is made into knitwear by famous brands. The Italian mills are also renowned for using cashmere and developing new qualities in the yarn. The colours obtained are exquisite, sometimes small amounts of shiny Lurex yarn or little sequins are mixed in to give it an extra lift. High-quality cashmere lasts for years, retaining both its softness and colour, so it's a purchase that you can expect to keep.

Cashmere knitwear, Scottish luxury

Long, soft fibres are essential for producing luxury cashmere knitwear, which is often treasured by its owners for years; these garments stand the test of time. Shorter fibres, sometimes used for lower-priced garments, tend to matt together over time and are not as robust as the high-quality luxury cashmere used in these cardigans by Hawick Cashmere. Picture courtesy of Textiles Scotland.

Pure, luxury cashmere can be both felt and seen, so before you make a purchase make sure the quality of the garment is high. While luxury cashmere is not cheap, it represents very good value.

The magic of cashmere colour

Scotland is synonymous with cashmere, having world famous knitwear brands and also high-class spinners and yarn manufacturers such as Todd & Duncan who source their yarn from China, and carry out the spinning and dyeing processes in Scotland. These processes are very complicated and require specialist knowledge.

Cashmere is renowned for the beauty of the colours that can be produced each season, an array of sophisticated tonal alchemy forming part of the enduring appeal of luxury cashmere, and striking a chord with customers in sophisticated international markets. Its ability to take colour exceptionally well is a key advantage of cashmere over other yarns.

Promoting Scottish cashmere

Cashmere is associated with luxury and style. Here a bespoke Claire McInally dress using 100 per cent Scottish Cashmere from Alec Begg was photographed as part of a high profile promotion to the US on behalf of the Scottish textile industry by Textiles Scotland. Scotland still produces a large amount of high-quality cashmere yarn fabric and clothing. This is a major attraction for the many designers who source their fabrics, colours and inspiration from the country. Scottish cashmere products are sold all over the world.

Cashmere, the Italian love affair

In this picture the approach to delicate colouration and fineness of yarn particularly characteristic of Italy is obvious. More cashmere is worn in Italy than anywhere else. Spinners at this level drive design, grouping yarns and colours to provide a coherent and creative direction for their customers. Many Italian companies are heavily involved in the Made in Italy label, which guarantees the origin of their designs, stressing the localism of their products and their connection to the area and workforce.

This cashmere is by Cariaggi, who are among the most renowned Italian yarn specialists. Their products are used by the top designers in many different countries. Cariaggi, still run by the family, prides itself on its long history, and it has revived Guado, or woad, the traditional natural blue dye of the district.

Cariaggi's A New Look for cashmere

Also by Italian spinner and fashion leader, Cariaggi, this is a new look. As well as the finest yarn, cashmere can also be spun in a thicker quality, reflecting the fashion for luxury higher-gauge garments with a more chunky feel that retains its softness. This bi-coloured yarn is much thicker than conventional cashmere and will be used for outer garments and chunky sweaters.

Scottish cashmere – soft and bright

Scottish cashmere knitters and weavers work with designers and buyers from prestigious brands who seek out Scottish cashmere, which is reputed to have a particular softness. Many yarn and fabric labels are well known in their own right. These examples show the range of colours which can be achieved.

Johnstons of Elgin is a Scottish cashmere specialist with an international reputation for its creative approach to design and the very high quality of its products, which includes knitwear and accessories often made from its own yarn. It has been in business since 1797 on the banks of the River Lossie.

Scottish mill Alexander Begg Cashmere specialises in accessories which can be seen on many a catwalk during Fashion Week. This collection of jewel colours demonstrates deep, rich cashmere used for scarves and throws, often mixed with silk for ultralight luxury.

Alpaca

Alpaca fleece is as soft as cashmere but lighter in weight. It is also strong and warm, used for knitwear as well as suits, coats and in blends with many other fibres. It gives fabrics a soft feel and a downy appearance and is almost always mixed with other yarns. When blended with wool or other fibres, alpaca gives them a unique texture and lightness.

Alpaca is associated mainly with South America, especially Peru, but also with New Zealand where there are large flocks of the goats in mountainous areas. There's a trend developing for small-scale alpaca farmers all over Europe and the States. These farmers are rearing them carefully and organically, often giving names to each animal. This is probably due to the fact the animals have individual faces with different expressions. Alpacas live best in a temperate climate, but they can also withstand cold winters, growing a warm and protective layer that is prized for fashion and practicality. Unlike wool, alpaca fibre doesn't have lanolin in it, so it has a dry feel.

Peruvian Alpaca fashion at Pitti Filati
Today many designers of luxury fabric and fashion, such as Giorgio Armani, use Suri alpaca to give extra softness and texture to men's and women's suits. Most alpaca is commercially produced in Peru, where it originated and was once kept for the exclusive use of the kings and rulers. There is a huge growth in small producers in the UK, USA and New Zealand, who form cooperatives to market and process the fleeces.

Mills in Bradford first experimented with commercial alpaca over a hundred years ago, but found it difficult to weave after it was first exported from South America to Europe. The most successful was the pioneering entrepreneur Titus Salt of Salts Mill in Saltaire, West Yorkshire (now a World Heritage Site) who developed the cloth successfully for formal suits.

Camel hair

Camel hair, with its distinctive gingery colour, has come back into fashion, where it is woven into very lightweight yet hard-wearing fabric for smart coats and jackets. A camel hair coat was a staple of men's and women's wardrobes for formal wear throughout most of the 20th century and is now being seen in all sorts of designer collections appealing to people who see it as new and different, if they can afford it. Camel hair overcoats for men can still be found in vintage shops usually styled in a generous way; long, raglan-sleeved and often belted.

Alpacas — better than dogs

Alpaca fleece is a natural animal fibre which can be either light or heavy, depending on the spinning. The wool is hypoallergenic. Alpaca is also naturally water-repellent and difficult to ignite. There are two breeds of alpaca, the Huacaya and the Suri. The Huacaya grows a soft spongy fibre with a natural crimp or curl, making a naturally elastic yarn, well suited for knitting. The Suri has less crimp and tends to be used for woven fabrics. This picture is one of the Flagstaff Alpacas from Dunedin, New Zealand; their fleece is used for clothing and furnishing.

Alpacas are closely related to llamas, and have been used recently to guard flocks of sheep in Yorkshire, which are troubled by foxes and other predators. In the United States, farmers are using alpacas as guards for pregnant ewes and newborn lambs, to protect them from coyote attacks. Alpacas are claimed to need a shorter training time than dogs.

Natural Peruvian alpaca yarn

Alpacas originated in the Andes where it is hot by day and very cold by night. The animals grow a thick, soft coat to keep them warm and it is this soft, crimped hair which is used for fabric making. Alpaca is often combined with wool when woven.

Children wearing PEA

PEA stands for Pure English Alpaca. There are many examples of pure alpaca from specialist producers on the market, showing the small-scale rearing of these attractive animals by committed farmers in various countries, especially the US, New Zealand, and increasingly the UK. These garments show knits including cardigans, sweaters and other knitted styles which are soft, light and wear very well. The softness makes it an ideal fabric for sensitive skin and small children.

Alpaca fleece is spun and made into a wide range of garments, from very simple and inexpensive clothes made by people working in small communities, to sophisticated and expensive, industrially made products. You may find there are small amounts of alpaca in all sorts of fashion garments, from formal clothes to knits, if you are curious enough to read the sewn-in fibre content label. Always a good thing to do!

A cria (baby alpaca)

This baby alpaca, called a cria, is one of the Flagstaff Alpacas from Dunedin, New Zealand. It is displaying some of the natural colours that make alpaca such an attractive natural fibre. There are 22 fleece colours recognised by the textile industry, in various shades ranging from white to brown. Alpaca is most often used in its undyed, natural colours, which can include very rich, dark shades. You are likely to find natural alpaca in good quality organic and eco brand labels.

Vicuña

Vicuña is commonly regarded as the most expensive fibre in the world, though there is nothing common about the precious fibre from the goat-like creature, the vicuña. It originates from South America, and was the sole prerogative of Mayan royalty when explorers and colonists from Europe first came across it. Vicuña, the smallest of the Camelid family, are an endangered species. The fibres derived from the vicuña are the finest capable of being spun into yarn and are softer, lighter and warmer than any other wool.

Vicuña has always been a status symbol, with a precious few hairs woven into sumptuously light and lustrous suiting fabric or tailored couture, dresses for wealthy women from Victorian times onwards. Italian mills, British weavers and their customers have always been very taken by the charms of this rare fibre and it has had a prestige and rarity value which justify its high price.

Today it is still used for expensive and exclusive fabrics made up into suits, sometimes in pure 100 per cent qualities, but often mixed with other animal fibres like wool. It is the ultimate in expensive suiting. Vicuña is woven by a very few specialist mills, mostly in Italy or the UK, and sold particularly to businessmen and CEOs of global companies, actors and politicians who desire the fabric because of its fineness and soft handle as the ultimate mark of success

Vicuña goats in the wild in Peru

The most expensive suitings in the world are made of pure 100 per cent vicuña. Prestigious tailors such as Dege and Skinner in Savile Row will sell some suits of vicuña each season to the few customers who choose and can afford such a luxury product, which performs remarkably well for such a light and soft fibre.

Vicuña wool is heavily certified to guarantee it is the genuine article. The animals are guarded in their enclaves in Peru since they are prey to poachers. It became illegal in the 1970s to trade in vicuña, but in 1993 that changed and the trade is now controlled by the Peruvian government.

Vicuña is also used in blends with other fibres and is selected for accessories, luggage and headwear for well-known labels like Borsalino and Ferragamo.

Vicuña was reportedly discovered by Christopher Columbus in the 1500s during his conquest of South America, where it had been exclusively reserved for the use of the Inca kings, and said to be more precious than gold and silver. It's a claim which can still be substantiated, weight for weight.

Cervelt

Cervelt is the soft hair combed from a red deer's winter coat. It is extremely precious as very little hair is obtained in the process. But when it is collected, the hairs are long, soft and lustrous and make fabrics which are shiny, luxurious and very exclusive.

Cervelt is a relatively new, expensive fibre, which has only recently been developed because of the difficulty of obtaining and processing the hair. Developed by Douglas Creek, it comes from New Zealand where there are millions of red deer reared in the South Island. The fibre can be used for both knitting and weaving and is proving durable and versatile. In its natural state, it has shades ranging from pale beige to deep red, and takes dye extremely well. Look out for it; you'll find it in luxury socks, scarves and accessories; Cervelt is on the way up, if you are.

Deer fibre bounds into fashion

Cervelt is the latest comer into the luxury fibre panoply. New Zealand might be renowned for the fact that sheep outnumber humans, but there are also a fair few red deer in the country. In fact, 2.5 million of them, which is one to every two human inhabitants. The long soft hairs are combed from the necks of red deer in the winter, a long but worthwhile process which yields small amounts of the precious hair. The fabrics repel water and have beautiful natural colourings ranging from red to dark brown, the red deer colour. They dye well into bright tones as well, and can be knitted or woven. Cervelt is used for upmarket accessories and luggage, hats and hosiery, scarves and sweaters, as well as fabrics for jackets and skirts with an exclusive tag.

For the ultimate in luxury socks, Cervelt red deer hair is knitted by Italian company De Pio into a subtle but precious status symbol.

Water droplets suspended on Cervelt

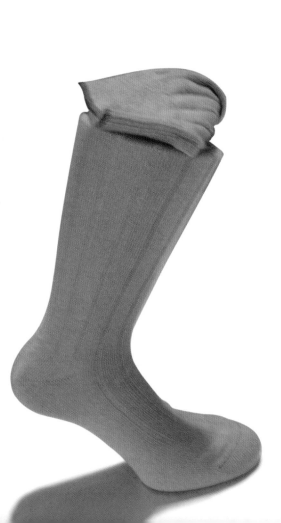

The ultimate luxury sock in Cervelt by De Pio, Italy

MOHAIR

MOHAIR has been prized as a precious fibre for centuries. Its sheen and colourful nature give it a certain allure that has been recognised by those who want to show off. In modern times it's been knitted into bulky, airy knits in bright colours and woven into cloth with a lustre that has caught the eye of princes and spivs alike.

Undoubtedly one of the prettiest and most appealing animals whose hair we use is the Angora goat. The goats are combed twice a year for their soft and lustrous curly hair. Mohair, which is made from those hairs, is durable, warm, extremely lightweight and lustrous with a soft hand. It is often combined with other fibres. Over 50 per cent of the world's production is in South Africa and the fibre and yarn are exported all over the world. New Zealand is also a producer of mohair.

The finest grade of mohair is kid mohair, obtained from the first shearing of a young Angora goat. Kid mohair is a recognised grade of fibre and it possesses the unique feature of natural wicking properties that draw perspiration away from the skin, preventing bacterial build up and odour.

Mohair suits are indelibly allied in the public mind with the Teddy Boys and rockers of the 1950s with a sort of showy Italian chic that came across to Britain together with coffee bars and pointed shoes, Lambretta and Vespa scooters. It's a look which is back in vogue.

Mohair fabric for suits had another revival when the punk movement spat its noisy way onto the cultural stage in the 1980s, and the shiny, strutting clash groups flaunted high-cost, shiny clothing which is now highly sought after in vintage clothing shops. The pop world has rediscovered mohair. Yorkshire specialist weavers of mohair are being asked to recreate the skinny shiny suit fabrics which marked out the uniform of the pop world for two generations.

It is also woven into far more subtle fabrics with a slight sheen, sometimes blended with other animal fibres to be used in bespoke suits and stylish womenswear. The weaving of mohair is a specialist art by mills such as Luxury Fabrics/William Halstead. The remaining mills which can do it export their fabrics to the Middle East, Japan and all over the world. Mohair can be woven into smooth suitings and also brushed into shaggy, hairy cloth for outerwear.

Mohair knitwear is soft and with its dramatic shiny look and fluffy feel is a hit with womenswear designers and their customers.

Which luxury suiting was worn by mods and punks and also is worn by bankers in international stock exchanges?

Mohair goats – the prettiest goats of all

Mohair comes from the Angora goat and more than 60 per cent of the fibre is produced in South Africa, with the US being the second most important producer. Though not as soft as cashmere, mohair has been highly valued across the centuries for its long fibres with lustrous, light-reflecting qualities, which makes a very lightweight and warm garment.

Cones of mohair yarn

These are cones of spun mohair yarn. The Angora goats are combed twice a year for their soft and lustrous hair. In South Africa it is a major industry and mohair is also cultivated in the US. It is a high-value fibre which is only found in the best quality clothes.

African mohair fashion

Mohair South Africa is managing to slow a decline in the rearing of mohair goats by streamlining production and offering a better price to farmers as the unique fibre is now greatly in demand for fashion internationally. Mohair has a high profile on the international catwalks, as well as being sought out in vintage shops.

Bright colours and fluffy yarn can be seen in these delicate lacy knits by African Expressions, made from South African mohair. Mohair from South Africa is exported to expert knitters in Italy, Switzerland and China. Mohair is one of the most highly prized precious fibres. It is versatile and used in many different garments and has inspired many designers to exploit its special colour and texture. This is a truly specialist trade as it requires knowledgeable buyers to identify the best yarns and expertise to weave the yarns. The British weavers in Yorkshire are acknowledged masters of the art.

The brilliance of mohair

Mohair can also be hairy and comfortable, it takes dye exceptionally well and is a good insulator. Plus it doesn't crease. A classic luxury fibre, it is usually more expensive than most wool.

Womenswear designs and knitwear often use brushed mohair dyed with jewel colours, which gives a startlingly rich look, made up into sweaters, jackets and coats. This can give a very retro look which ties in with the current trend for vintage fashion. These brilliant designs are by Samuel Tweed, based in Yorkshire in northern England, demonstrate the attraction of this dramatic fibre.

Outdoor fashion in mohair

Mohair has been around as a precious fibre for centuries and the word mohair has been used in English since the 1500s. It's been used for knitting into bulky airy knits in bright colours, but it is also used for weaving into more formal cloth with a lustre and sheen that can be sophisticated and subtle, or shiny and flamboyant.

A mohair suit does not come cheap, and it's teamed up with high-quality wool to make a sophisticated and shiny fabric. A mohair suit is at the same time classy and also a bit edgy, especially when worn by musicians and people wanting to make a style statement. The examples above are made from lightweight 60% kid mohair and 40% Super 100s wool by John Foster.

Skinny mohair suits were the iconic shiny fabrics worn by mods and punks. Mohair suiting is an elite fabric chosen by people in power the world over, its shine conveying class and luxury.

RIGHT *Knitted mohair, African Expressions*

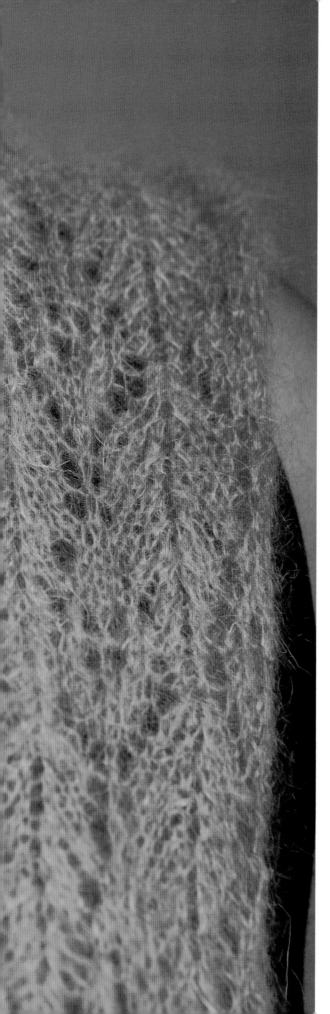

Dinner jacket of mohair/wool 007 style

Pure mohair and blends are the mark of the universal image of sophistication — the dinner suit, with the quintessential suave image established by James Bond.

Pop stars in the 1950s and 60s made mohair fashionable with a more iconoclastic look, choosing exceptionally shiny fabrics and skinny silhouettes which became the signature look of some punk bands. Now mohair is newly fashionable, as its lustre reflects the current fashion for shine. Younger designers are using mohair and you will find mohair content in knitwear, skirts, suits and coats. It is often used in fibre blends to add its particular qualities to the mix.

SILK

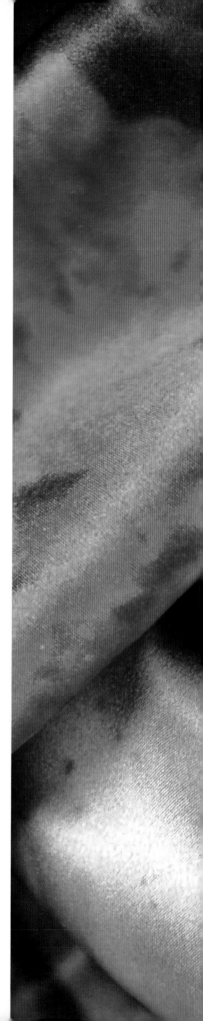

IT'S always a marvel to realise that thousands of cocoons from a small worm can yield up a fibre that is spun into one of the most ancient and luxurious fabrics in the world. The enduring attraction of pure silk is its shine, iridescence, lightness and strength — qualities that it lends to any fibres it is added to. When blended with wool, or twisted with linen, silk gives the cloth a subtle light and seems to 'lift' the colours contained in the weave. On its own it shimmers, catches the light and changes its colour, being lightweight and soft to wear.

Silk has been traded for centuries and is one of the fabrics to have had an impact on the growth of civilisations. The 'Silk Road' still describes the route along which silk was traded from the time of the Han Dynasty, from China to Europe, via Afghanistan and on to the Mediterranean, opening up corridors from East to West. The route linked different cultures and contributed to their economic growth. The importance of both the fibre and the fabric is thus more than simply aesthetic.

Silk can be classed as an animal product. The larvae are grown in their millions mainly in the Far East to supply the continuing demand for fashion. The casing of the cocoons which house the silk grubs is carefully unwound to reveal the threads that are spun into the fine, light and strong yarn. This yarn is used in fabrics in all types of luxury clothing from underwear to coats. Unfortunately, the silk worms perish in this process. Recently there has been research and development of a 'vegetarian' form of silk which allows the moths to survive, by a complicated and expensive process, but this is a tiny part of the market.

There is another animal which produces silk, the spider. Recently a lustrous golden jacquard patterned silk fabric was

What creature produces silk, apart from silkworms?

It's the spider.

Lustrous agate silk scarf designed by Richard Weston, who specialises in designs captured from nature and natural materials such as minerals, fossils and rocks

Silk is a precious, natural fibre, one which most people are likely to come across and buy, whether for a silk tie, scarf, blouse, shirt or dress. Silk is also used in blends with many other fibres. Silk is intimately associated with cultures of the East, Japan, China and India where its colour and lustre are particularly valued. Designers flirt with silk to display their ideas translated into overt opulence. Weaves are bright and silk prints legendary. Newer digital prints on silk can produce realist pictures of photographic intensity.

exhibited in London and New York made from woven spider's web silk. Its creation demanded thousands of hours of work: 70 people spent four years collecting golden orb spiders in Madagascar and carefully extracting about 80 feet of silk filament from each of the arachnids. The spiders are not killed in the process. It astonished visitors, but looks unlikely to be adopted as a conventional material, though the spiders only take about a week to replace the extracted silk. Web silk has astonishing tensile strength too which is exciting physicists and engineers; if it could be translated into ropes it would be stronger than steel, a thin strand being able to hold up suspension bridges.

Conventional silk fabric is sumptuous when dyed in deep jewel colours, showing off its natural slub, or irregularity, and as such has been the stuff of the rich and the powerful for thousands of years, dressing themselves in showy silk garments, flaunting their standing and influence.

These days, most people will have some items of real silk in their wardrobe. Mass production of the silk worms means it is within the reach of those who want to choose a beautifully flattering fabric to impress, whether Hollywood's ball gowns designed by couture names or satin wedding dresses in ceremonies across the world. Pure silk scarves, dresses and shirts are readily available and a percentage of silk is found in many jackets and suits for summer fashion.

Silk is particularly prized in the East; Japanese, Indian and Chinese cultures have put silk at the centre of their rituals and ceremonies, their appreciation of colour and decoration finding an expression in this most lustrous and beautiful of fabrics.

Printed silk

This printed silk by Lanre da Silva Ajaye, Lagos Fashion Week, exploits the colour and sheen of this fibre. Silk can be smooth as satin and can also be woven so that natural irregularities of the yarn are retained, giving extra texture. Silk is often found in alternative collections, alongside organic and eco fabrics. Silk underwear and lingerie are the top choice for luxury brands.

Woven spider's silk

This woven golden garment is made from spider's silk and was on show at the Victoria & Albert Museum in London. It involved thousands of hours of collection and painstaking weaving. Various arachnids produce silk which is exciting the attention of scientists, since its tensile strength is exceptional.

For textiles, spider silk is unlikely to hit the mainstream, but it shows how the industry's fascination with innovation and exploration, such as how exotic materials might be adapted for apparel, has driven it over centuries of inventive projects.

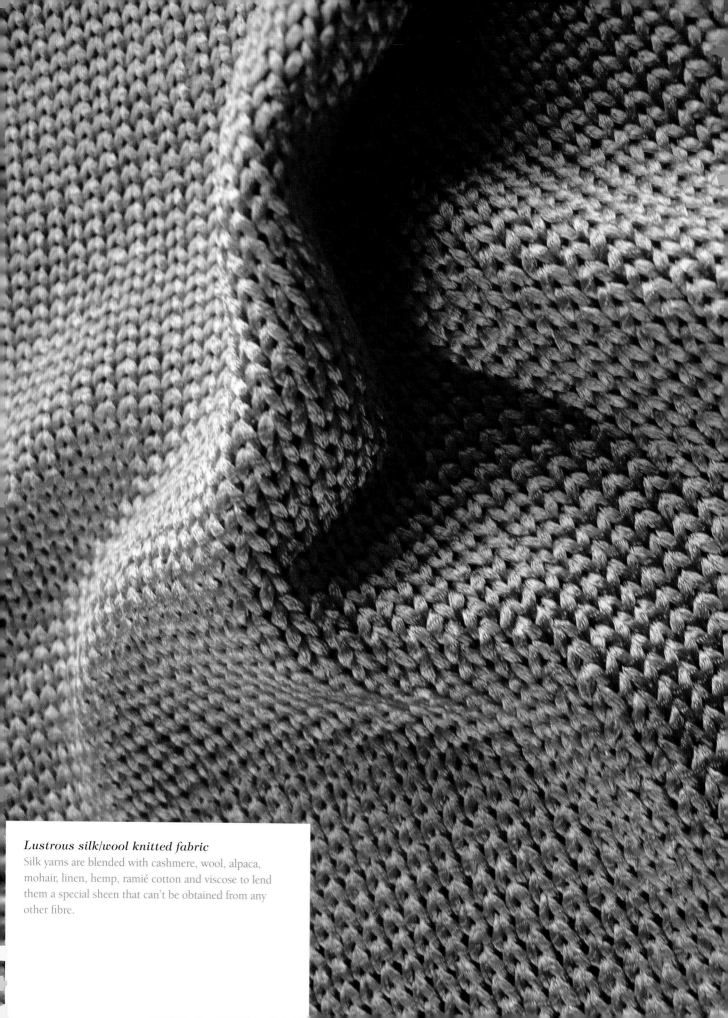

Lustrous silk/wool knitted fabric

Silk yarns are blended with cashmere, wool, alpaca, mohair, linen, hemp, ramié cotton and viscose to lend them a special sheen that can't be obtained from any other fibre.

Winning design by Ying Wu,
Texprint, 2012

Texprint an annual competition, brings together the crème de la crème of graduate textile designers studying in the UK . The beautiful colours and graphic print in this winning design make the most of the lustrous silk. Silk prints often attain the status of art and, of course, silk-screen prints are themselves sometimes framed and exhibited, or used as wall hangings. Pucci print silk scarves are heirlooms treasured by their wearers and handed on.

Irridescent silk caftan

Silk fibre has the ability to absorb moisture and, being closely woven, it is also warm to wear next to the skin but it's also almost weightless, ideal for summer. Today silk can be found at all levels of the market, used for light, soft and shiny tops, skirts and trousers, shirts and blouses, saris and kaftans. For knitwear, silk is often paired with luxury fibres like cashmere or as a component of fine wool jackets and tweeds, always lending its sparkle and light to the garment.

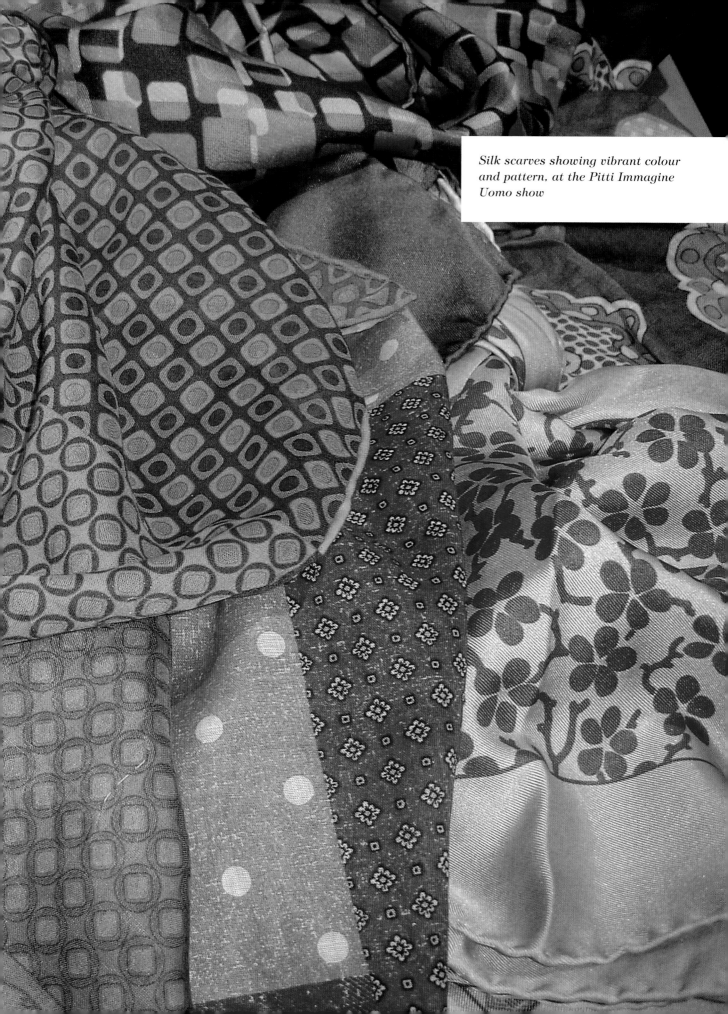

Silk scarves showing vibrant colour and pattern, at the Pitti Immagine Uomo show

2

Plant fibres

Plant fibres

There are more fabrics made from plant fibre worn in the world than cloth made from animal fibre. Humans have used plants for cloth ever since they started settling in one place and planting things, and weaving was probably the earliest technology invented. Techniques have developed in almost every society to process plant stems, leaves and flowers for wearing. Fibre plants are often abundant, but they rely on the sun, rain and a lot of labour to grow and harvest them. These factors still remain variables that must be taken into account.

Cotton and linen are the most frequently used plant fibres, but many more plants are being investigated for their suitability for textiles such as nettles, soya, tobacco, corn, hemp, bamboo and jute. They have the advantage of being very fast growing, though there is often competition for the fashion industry these days from the growing demand for bio-fuels.

Wearing plants is a bit like eating food. Both areas are subject to vigorous debates about how their production should be managed. For example, should genetic modification (GM) be involved to breed plants which are genetically reliable and suited to particular environments? And should ecological principles be brought into play, for example avoiding chemicals and additives, which might result in cheaper products but of a lower quality? Certainly, in fashion there is a real move towards better quality clothes underpinned by high-quality fabrics. The ideas about Slow Food are neatly echoed by the Italians' idea of Slow Fashion – high-quality produce with excellent ingredients.

Which plant fibre is found in almost every place where there are humans?

Cotton is the universal fabric, found in almost every place where there are humans. It is used for weaving blue jeans and knitting T-shirts, modern humankind's uniform.

COTTON

COTTON was one of the first fibres to be grown exclusively for clothing. Remnants of cotton textiles dating from approximately 3600 BC have been found in Mexico and other early examples have been found in other countries throughout the world. Today it is a vitally important crop in many countries where it is hot and wet enough for the irrigation required, and where there is enough acreage to support vast fields of cotton plants; the Middle East, notably Egypt where it was probably first cultivated, India and Pakistan, Turkey, Greece, China, the Southern States of the USA, West Indies and South America.

Cotton is a vegetable fibre with white lint-bearing fluffy flowers that are harvested, combed and spun into yarn that is used for almost every item of clothing. If you think about the millions of pairs of jeans and T-shirts that are worn every day around the world by everyone from students to chic designers, it's easy to see why cotton is the most widely worn natural fibre on earth.

Scientists have turned their attention to improving cotton performance, and it benefits from technical advances such as water-repellent and non-iron finishes. Wicking treatments that draw moisture from the body to the outside of the fabric

Bright stripes and checks Italian style
Pitti Immagine Uomo, the most important menswear show, held twice a year in Florence, brings thousands of buyers from different countries to the Fortezza da Basso to choose the styles they will buy for their stores for the following season. These Paul & Shark cotton shirts were in a recent Pitti Uomo and show the bright colours of traditional madras checked cottons. The trendy label, and many of the other well-known brands at the exhibition, have their own flagship stores in Italy, as well as selling to up-market boutiques internationally. They foster a relaxed, stylish look for men.

Many cotton fabrics are treated to require minimum ironing, especially the more luxury products. This is another example of why it is often more sensible to choose a better quality fabric that makes garments worth their purchase price. Basically, the more information that's offered about the fabric, the better the quality will be.

prevent uncomfortable chafing. Special construction and finishes, allow cotton to dry much more quickly.

The downside has been that cotton requires pesticides and water to be grown successfully, and bleaching after it's harvested. Sustainable cotton is the big breakthrough, using fewer pesticides. Since 1996, the Sustainable Cotton Project has supported sustainably grown cotton fibre. In the field the project works with innovative growers to produce a high-quality fibre without using the most toxic pesticides and herbicides. It connects growers, manufacturers and consumers to develop a Cleaner Cotton™ supply chain. This initiative has been very successful and a growing number of fashion retailers and major brands have a stated goal of only using sustainable cotton.

Organic cotton is a more expensive option but it has great attraction for eco-minded consumers, particularly in Germany, the US and Scandinavia where there is an enthusiastic younger customer who is keen to buy organic cotton, certified free of additives and grown under strictly controlled conditions. In other developments, genetically modified (GM) crops have been developed which need less water. This quest for improvement chimes with the public mood.

Cotton's inherent softness and absorption has made it the traditional choice for bodywear and underwear, babywear and sportswear. It's soft and very easy to wear, it has natural stretch, absorbs more moisture than synthetic fibres and it wears well.

It comes in a range of different qualities determined by the length of the fibre or staple. Luxury cotton with long threads, or staple, is branded at a premium, like Sea Island cotton from the West Indies, Pima and Supima varieties from Egypt and the US and Makò from the Americas are used particularly for smart city shirts.

The yarn can be woven into thicker canvas heavy weights, as well as light, technical fabrics, and is blended with all sorts of partners like polyester, viscose, nylon or wool and cashmere, often with stretch yarns. It is also teamed up with linen, silk or cashmere.

Jeans made of sturdy cotton denim (named after the city of Nimes where it was first woven for hardwearing work wear) were the first important branded goods, with customers often staying loyal to their own particular favourite label for a lifetime. Cotton denim fashion is constantly renewed and different finishes like stone washing, bleaching, slashing, distressing or fading become more complex every season. Sustainable denim is a major movement by manufacturers of the fabric, reducing the chemical content of processing and choosing responsibly cultivated cotton.

Cotton is the preferred fabric worn in hotter climates, but it can now be blended with animal fibres and various different techno finishes so that it can be worn in colder weather. People like the feel of cotton, and as the second most important fibre in the world, it's still a hard act to beat.

Fine cotton shirting

This fine cotton shirting with classic gingham check in the shirtmaker's favourite, sky blue and white, shows a typical 'posh' work shirt fabric. Very long staple cotton is used where the threads are continuous and can be woven into a smooth, sophisticated fabric for this type of upmarket shirt. Often made to measure, it is also used by quality brands and sourced in the West Indies, South America or Egypt. This type of shirting cotton is treated to be non-shrink and can be laundered easily. It is the sort of fabric used by top shirtmakers in London's Jermyn Street and by menswear designer brands in Italy. It will be seen in Wall Street and the City of London, where standards of dressing in a bold and luxurious way go with the territory. The example above is from DJA, part of the Albini Group in Italy.

Gathering cotton in the fields

This picture of cotton being harvested in Egypt is representative of the way that the fabric you gaily buy in a store will often have travelled halfway around the world. It might be cashmere from the harsh uplands of Mongolia or China, or cotton grown in the hot climates of India, Pakistan, the West Indies or South America. Cotton comes in different qualities according to the length of the fibre or staple. Cotton with long threads, or staple, is branded as premium, like Sea Island cotton from the West Indies or Pima and Mako cotton from North and South America. This luxury fibre is used in high fashion garments, casual wear, sportswear and top quality garments like classic shirts because it gives a cleaner, smoother line and can be woven more easily.

The cotton plant and the futures market

As it grows, the white lint of the flowers blankets the vast fields in clouds. Cotton is particularly dependent on rainfall. Droughts can decimate the crop so irrigation is a necessity. It is why in ancient times cotton was originally grown in the Nile Delta where the mighty river regularly flooded. Today the crop is still dependent on rainfall, and if a major drought affects the growing regions the price fluctuations will be reflected in the price of clothes.

This is why the fashion trade keeps a weather eye on climate as well as economic conditions. The industry has also pushed for measures to ensure more sustainable manufacturing. Most raw materials are traded like other commodities, with traders buying at judicious moments to get the best price for the manufacturers who in turn build up long-term economic ties with countries and growers.

Cotton growing in the fields

Cotton is a vitally important crop in many countries: The middle east, notably Egypt where it seems to have been first cultivated, India and Pakistan, Turkey, Greece, the southern United States and South America. These are countries where it is hot and wet enough for the substantial irrigation required, and where there is enough acreage to support vast fields of cotton plants. Cotton is an attractive fluffy plant, but in the 19th century the lint was responsible for long-term respiratory problems for the mill workers. But thankfully this is no longer true due to modern manufacturing methods and health and safety measures.

Long staple cotton equals high-quality underwear

Scientists across the world have turned their attention to improving the performance of cotton. One of the greatest advances has been moisture management, reducing the effects of perspiration on fabrics, reducing sweaty odours and drying the fabric more quickly to reduce rubbing particularly important for activewear. Cotton is soft and absorbent, but this absorbency can be too much if you're exercising in cold weather. Wicking Windows® or Transdry® has been developed by Cotton Incorporated, the US-based company charged with the research and promotion of cotton. It allows 100% cotton fabrics to transfer moisture away from the skin. The treatment reduces chafing from wet fabric and it dries 50% faster than non-treated cotton. Limitless fabric combinations of untreated cotton and TransDry® treated wicking cotton can be constructed to add drying performance to any garment so cotton can compete in the gym and sports with any synthetic.

OPPOSITE *Washed and aged denim looks at Denim by PV*

There are more denim jeans worn in the world than any other garment. Hardwearing and robust, the word for these trousers comes from 'serge de Nîmes', Nîmes being the town in France where denim was first produced for workmen. It took two hundred years for the style to become the uniform of every man and woman and the present-day garment is not far from the original, including rivets.

Denim is a major consumer of cotton, and almost a world in itself. Fashion and fabric expertise is extremely specialist: wool buyers judge the seasonal clip by hand and eye, cashmere traders disappear into the wilds of the mountainous regions of Kashmir and Mongolia for months to track down the finest and softest hair, and likewise designers and buyers of denim are extremely expert, often spending their whole career in this market, seeking out new effects, antiquing, bushing, stone washing and fraying the fabric to produce jeans which will meet the exigent standards of the denim lovers.

For this reason, there are now important specialist shows dedicated to denim, like Denim by PV, which takes place in Paris, and Denim by PV Asia, held in Shanghai, Munich Fabric Start, and other regional shows, which introduce the new colours, qualities and special effects we will see in the shops a year later.

Exhibitors range from new brands to massive labels like Levi, Wrangler, Pepe. The market is international and buoyant, but there is a constant quest for novelty in fit, fabric and style as the market is geared towards the young, where customers are constantly looking for something new.

RRING

supplier: LAVANDERIA
EMMETRE
stand: H 62
compo:

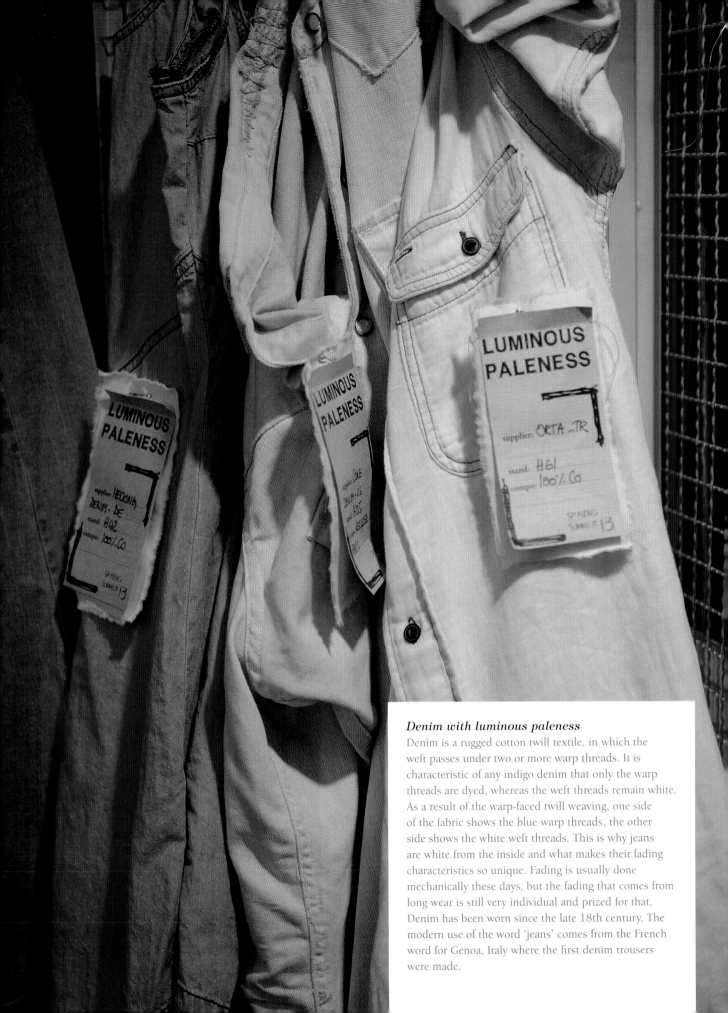

Denim with luminous paleness

Denim is a rugged cotton twill textile, in which the weft passes under two or more warp threads. It is characteristic of any indigo denim that only the warp threads are dyed, whereas the weft threads remain white. As a result of the warp-faced twill weaving, one side of the fabric shows the blue warp threads, the other side shows the white weft threads. This is why jeans are white from the inside and what makes their fading characteristics so unique. Fading is usually done mechanically these days, but the fading that comes from long wear is still very individual and prized for that. Denim has been worn since the late 18th century. The modern use of the word 'jeans' comes from the French word for Genoa, Italy where the first denim trousers were made.

ABOVE *Coloured denim*

RIGHT *Checked shirt and distressed jeans by Mark Thomas Taylor*

Coloured denim and blends with fibres like Tencel® have hit the market recently, for both men and women. Bright orange, yellow or purple denim as well as the classic blue which ranges from deep indigo to sky, and bleached out colours can now be found. The shapes that the connoisseurs in the stores will look for, such as the number of pockets, the cut (flares, cigarettes, bootleg, jeggings, etc.) and the height of the waist, are all specific to the season's trends.

Cotton has a glamour side. Over the ages cotton has been fashioned into sophisticated fine lawn, lace and muslin as well as everyday undergarments and nightwear. Wealthy people who could afford rare and beautiful costumes kept their finely embroidered and exquisitely woven cottons and handed them on as heirlooms. Cotton is even used for ballgowns and wedding dresses.

ABOVE *Cotton is on the way up with Judy R Clark designs*

LEFT *The Cotton Bride*

Cotton lace – revival of the craft

Cotton lace is more and more popular, and MYB Textiles in Scotland is famous for its lace making. A traditional firm in its quality standards, it has invested heavily in design technology and modernisation to meet the needs of the evolving market place. In addition to their range of traditional Madras and Nottingham Lace looms, the company has recently harnessed 100-year-old looms with electronic jacquards. It has revived the reputation of Scottish lace.

The description 'Nottingham lace' is still used and reflects the English town's former reputation as the lace-making centre of the world during the British Empire. Some specialist lace manufacturing still survives and the world-famous Nottingham lace market is a real tourist attraction.

Cotton couture

Emmy Rossum in a red cotton dress featuring the actress/singer in a design by Monique Lhuillier.

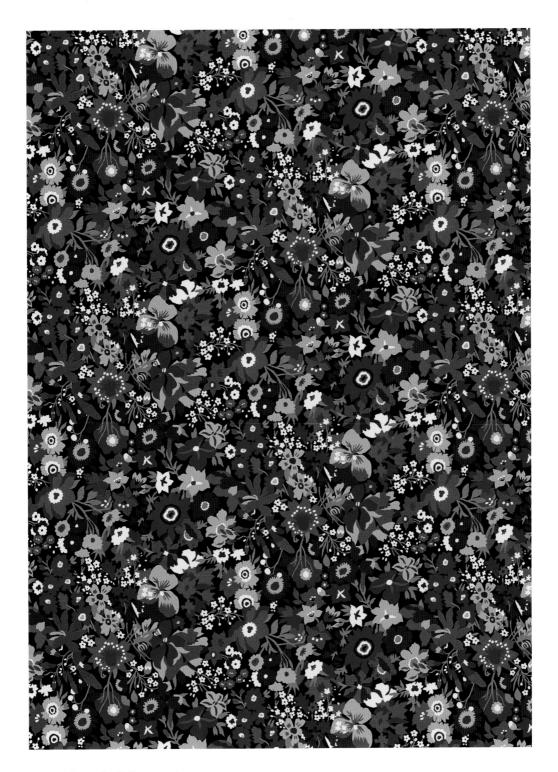

ABOVE *Manuela Liberty print*

OPPOSITE *Typical Liberty print on cotton,
Tana Lawn*

LINEN AND RAMIE

IF YOU'RE reading this in summer and you're interested in style, you're probably wearing linen in some form or another; a light natural-coloured jacket, a cool skirt dress or shirt, linen jeans, or perhaps some knitwear which is feather light but sophisticated and stylish.

Linen is one of the oldest fibres known to humankind: scraps of fabric in linen and hemp have been found in prehistoric burial sites. It is made from the fibres of the flax plant that grows profusely in wetter areas of the world. It's cultivated and processed mainly in northern Europe by companies that have been in business for generations. Linen is a strong, sturdy fabric that can protect as well as keeping the wearer warm. The fibres can also be woven into finer fabrics and diaphanous knits.

Ramie is a similar fibre, known as bast. Bast fibres such as ramie and flax derived from the inner bark of certain plants. Ramie, also called China grass, is a flowering plant related to the nettle and native to eastern Asia. For centuries, ramie fibre has been used for making fabrics and clothing — in fact, since at least 5000-3000 BC in Egypt. Ramie fibres are one of the strongest natural fibres, up to eight times stronger than cotton, and ramie does not shrink. Other types of nettles, from the same family, are also used for clothing, and have strong eco credentials.

Linen is the most useful and widespread of these bast fibres. Yarns and fabrics made from linen can be so fine and soft that you may not even know you're wearing linen. When spun very fine, it can be knitted into delicate cardigans and T-shirts that can be layered to cope with the temperature. In its fine, gauzy state it flows and is semi-transparent, but still retains a dry crunchy feel that marks it out from other fibres. But complex spinning and finishing techniques means it can also be used for shiny, resined raincoats as well as the softest floating voiles, fine knitwear or underwear.

What do you think of when you contemplate buying a linen shirt? The luxury of the feel against the skin, or the fact that someone has spent hours ironing the creases out of it? These days linen, more often than not, is easy-care, especially when it is blended with another fibre less prone to creasing or has elastic fibres so that it can spring back into shape.

Linen in its natural state

This is undyed, untreated linen, which looks and feels surprisingly like human hair. Linen is often used in its natural state in weaves, creating the ultimate fashionable eco effect. Linen is a 'green' fibre, requiring fewer chemicals in its production than any other fibre. It's also a fibre that can be used in its entirety for various purposes. As well as being a top fashion fabric, it can be incorporated as insulation in buildings and lately as fillings in cars; the automotive and aerospace industries are very interested in its qualities. In addition it's being developed as a lightweight component of items such as tennis racquets where it can cut down the weight substantially. Its strength makes it ideal for home furnishings as well as outerwear and now it can also be spun fine enough for underwear, lingerie and delicate gauzy blouses and dresses.

Relaxed linen fashion with a vintage soul from R 95th

Linen fabrics have the ability to look dressed up and casual at the same time. It's why it appeals to all ages. In its natural state linen shows the bumps and irregularities of the yarn, these 3-D effects give texture as well. Often teamed with cotton or denim, linen is used for cool summer jackets and trousers, dresses and skirts. If you're Italian you wear the creases with pride, a mark of genuine, 100% linen, if you're British or American you probably want it to look a bit smoother, with a treatment to reduce the creasing or the addition of a stretch yarn or another fibre. Fashionable sun-faded colours give just the right casual look to summer fashion for men and women.

Retting, laying down the flax in the fields

Linen is a repository of ancient words associated with the processing of the fibre. Scutching is the extraction of fibres from the flax plant stems. Retting, or rotting, happens when the stalks of linen are laid out to be processed naturally by the dual action of the sun and the rain. It was once the characteristic smell of the linen towns in Northern Ireland, where linen was produced until a decade ago. The fibres gradually soften, ready for bringing into the factories and processing into spinable fibres. It was said to smell strong, but not unpleasant.

Linen flax fields

The fields of flax with their pale blue flowers are one of the great sights in Flanders, Belgium, northern France and the Low Countries, attracting coach parties of tourists who come to admire them and stop off at the chic factory shops of the linen companies on the way. The country areas and small towns near the coasts of northern Europe are still intimately associated with the linen trade, where the growing, retting, scutching, spinning and weaving into fabric take place.

Savile Row tailors have had a long tradition of choosing linen for summer jackets, showing off the natural slubs and irregularities in the yarn. It is also likely to turn up in the better ranges on the High Street.

One of the reasons for linen's enduring popularity is its combination of virtues. Linen has a long heritage, can be sustainably produced, uses fewer chemicals and pesticides than most other fibres, including cotton, and the processing is still largely mechanical and needs less water. Billed as an eco fabric, in-depth studies have demonstrated that in addition to requiring very little chemical addition in its cultivation, most of the plant is employed and the residue can be used for fertiliser. Modern consumers, concerned about the excessive use of resources, find the sustainable qualities of linen very appealing.

And, to add to its list of virtues, linen is thermo regulating. It can absorb or release up to 20 per cent of its weight in water, without feeling damp, which is why it has been used in hot climates for so long.

Soft and luxurious when blended with silk, linen is cool and draping with cotton, warm and fuzzy with wool, angora or cashmere, making it the favourite with designers experimenting with texture and shape. It can be dyed into deep, strong colours. But it is also prized in its raw, natural state, with irregularities in the weave giving every piece of fabric an individual character, its colour ranges from different shades of ecru through to yellow and brown. It is a mix of long-established tradition and constant innovation that keeps linen at the forefront of international fashion. The industry is constantly researching and developing ways to extend the range of its application. Linen is a smart fabric in both the old sense of the word and in the new high-tech meaning. It's associated with high quality and good taste. These days it's also the fabric of directional designs and surprising variations in the way it looks.

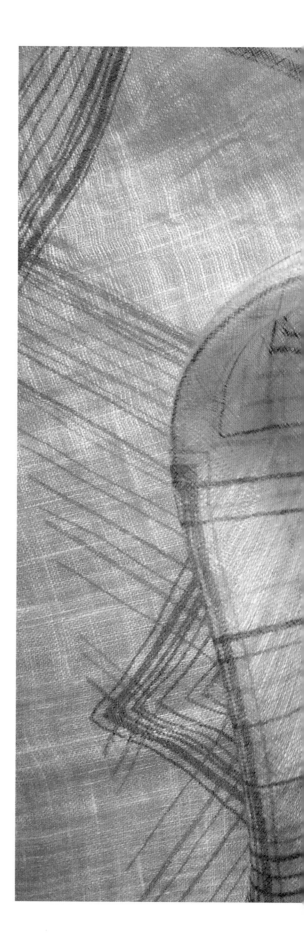

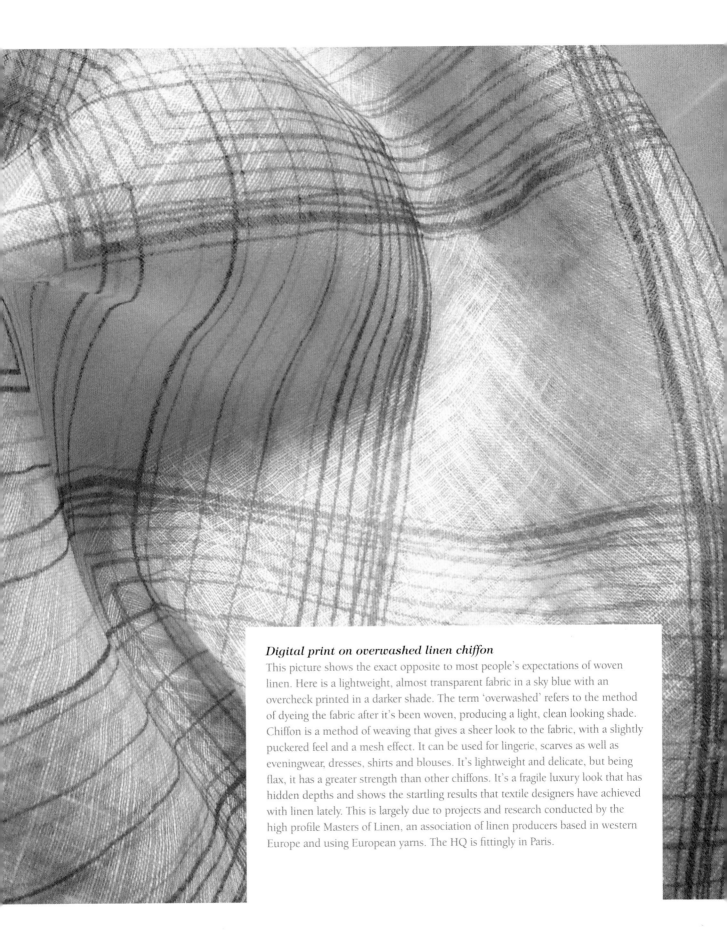

Digital print on overwashed linen chiffon

This picture shows the exact opposite to most people's expectations of woven linen. Here is a lightweight, almost transparent fabric in a sky blue with an overcheck printed in a darker shade. The term 'overwashed' refers to the method of dyeing the fabric after it's been woven, producing a light, clean looking shade. Chiffon is a method of weaving that gives a sheer look to the fabric, with a slightly puckered feel and a mesh effect. It can be used for lingerie, scarves as well as eveningwear, dresses, shirts and blouses. It's lightweight and delicate, but being flax, it has a greater strength than other chiffons. It's a fragile luxury look that has hidden depths and shows the startling results that textile designers have achieved with linen lately. This is largely due to projects and research conducted by the high profile Masters of Linen, an association of linen producers based in western Europe and using European yarns. The HQ is fittingly in Paris.

A row of summer suits at Pitti Immagine Uomo

Linen is the fabric of choice for summer suits, either in 100% or blends with cotton. Plain fabrics, gingham checks or seersucker looks are key for single-breasted jackets with matching or contrasting trousers. Glazed linen gives a sophisticated sheen for formal suits and dresses.

Some designers are exploring totally organic lines, with luxury linen from Normandy, that is woven in Italy and dyed with natural products such as indigo leaves, nuts, berries and tree bark, sourced from pioneering dyers who are located mainly in Italy and Holland.

The navy linen blazer or faded natural pale yellow linen jacket is an almost universal staple of men's formal wardrobes, worn by spectators at Lords cricket ground in London to smart young Italians strolling around the towns of Italy on a summer evening. The British Empire was founded on generations of men exiled to tropical climates wearing creased linen suits and solar topees (pith helmets). Similar styles are now made by Italian brands who have recognised their heritage value.

Linen mixed with wool and silk

Linen has been mainly a summer fabric until recently. Now, however, manufacturers such as Libeco in Belgium and Lanificio Botto in Italy are some of the weavers who have achieved the hard task of marrying together the different behaviours of linen and wool. Their success means that the handle and strength of linen is given the extra quality of warmth for colder weather by the addition of wool or cashmere. This sort of blend is very successful, making a flexible fabric which dyes well, such as this example in a rich pink, with an 'invisible' check, knitted in a soft jersey quality to be used for shirts, dresses and skirt designs. Linen can be blended with cotton, silk, cashmere and blends of all of these, to make it look or feel a certain way. With polyamide or polyester, Lurex or Lycra it can be sparkling, washable and stretchy too.

Water repellent linen raincoat

The reason why linen is so high profile among designers is because there is so much research and experiments with new treatments which are changing and improving its properties. Pret pour Partir is a French fashion company that has been working with technical linen developed in Italy. Linen has been coated to make it water repellent for summer showers, and given a Teflon finish on winter fabrics that can be used for winter raincoats. This would have been very rare not so long ago. Linen and hemp, which is produced in a similar way, are both used for luxury luggage by Céline, Balenciaga, Chanel making linen a total solution for travel.

Soft, light linen in nautical colours

European flax originates in a wide coastal band from Normandy to the Netherlands. Summer fashion is associated with the easy elegance of linen clothes for seaside holidays, strolling in Deauville on the Normandy coast, or the beaches of New Jersey. Bleached-out colours could be said to be associated with the breezy northern beaches, brighter, deeper coloured fabrics for holidays in Italy or the South of France. Libeco is a famous name in linen, a family firm in Belgium that is conscious of its eco credentials and firmly rooted in the rural economy where it's based. It produces elegant designs for clothing and also interiors, to be found in luxury stores worldwide.

OPPOSITE *Linen on the catwalk from Kenzo*

Linen is a star of the catwalk, used by designers like Stella McCartney for her casual chic style. She incorporated the fabric in a recent collection for jackets, shorts and blouses, dyed in a bright blue which is only found in linen. This is because, being a hollow fibre, the structure ensures it 'takes' dye exceptionally well. Kenzo, in this picture, has developed an outfit in blue linen with bright blue and white stripes.

Italian designers often opt for natural hues, for example Alberta Ferretti teamed knee length shorts with a peplum waisted jacket in natural linen. Gucci, Ferragamo, Etro, and Gianfranco Ferré epitomise the chic Italian approach to elegant linen fashion, with shades from beige to ginger and gold to dark brown.

Gaultier Bermuda shorts outfit

A twist on the image of a formal summer outfit is
shown in this Jean-Paul Gaultier linen suit with
Bermuda shorts and a tailored jacket for children.
Designers have recognised that childrenswear is
a major market for parents who are prepared to
spend money on children's outfits to complement
their own approach to dressing. The 'mini-me'
trend is international and echoed at all sorts of
stores. Quality clothes for children in the best
fabrics are selling well, and parents look at the
quality in the garments they are choosing. Whether
reacting to the excellence of natural fibres, the
purity of linen next to the skin, or the wish to
choose the best fabrics, linen seems to be firmly
on the wish list of parents. Linen is promoted as
having inherent qualities that are ideal for garments
which touch babies' skins.

Luxury linen fabrics

Dyed linen has a particular aesthetic effect, showing the weave and the tiny irregularities of the yarn. It is particularly suited to pale pinks, faded blues, light greens and also the bright white that, teamed with navy blue, sums up summer. These fabrics by Solbiati, the Italian linen specialists, will be made into jackets suits and shirts. The patterns echo traditional wool designs with windowpane checks, Prince of Wales checks and stripes. The plain or solid colours are pastels with a sunny look that is well suited to fashion shirts and blouses, trousers and shirts. 100% linen has a definite 'handle' or feel which is easily recognisable. Solbiati is the premier Italian linen mill.

Woven linen

This is linen as it looks when it is used for its natural qualities, in a simple knit, with the colour in a natural shade. Although woven linen has been in existence for thousands of years, linen in knits was unknown until fairly recently. The structure of the fibre made it difficult to spin yarns suitable for knitting. Now linen yarn has been made more malleable so that it can be looped and twisted for knitting. It is being used more and in different types of knits, from jersey to very fine delicate knits or blended with cotton or wool for hand-knitted jumpers.

Linen spinner Safilin is based in Northern France, where 70% of the world's linen is grown. Safilin has expert spinners of various types of linen yarn for different end-uses, including industrial products for insulation; another example of how every part of the linen plant is usable. Even the roots of the plant can be ploughed into the soil as fertiliser.

Linen shoe

Linen, being an elegant sort of fabric, has found its way on to a smart, urban shoe. With constructed soles, insoles and lacing, this shoe is a world away from the sports shoe or trainer. The linen is woven with classic stripes.

VISCOSE

IN THE past few years, if you have read the labels sewn into your clothes, you will have noticed that viscose is being used more frequently. You might not be able to feel it, as it can mimic cotton, but its main attraction is softness and the silky brightness of its colour range. It also takes prints exceptionally well. Viscose is used in light summer wear; dresses, skirts, blouses, shirts, knitwear, jackets and trousers. Blended with winter fibres, viscose can be worn in the colder weather as well.

Viscose is a manufactured fibre derived from nature. Many people don't realise that viscose is made from wood pulp. It is the most important of the cellulosic man-made fibres and has a long tradition. Another little-known fact is that rayon, the first successful manufactured fibre, was the forerunner of modern viscose. Over a century ago, it was discovered that cellulose fibres could be dissolved and reconstituted so that they could be spun and woven or knitted. The discovery came about as manufacturers looked for a way to create artificial silk as an alternative to expensive natural silk. The result was rayon.

Viscose is sourced from renewable tree bark taken from cultivated trees such as beech or pine. As a cellulosic fibre, it has come into its own because the quick growing trees from which it is sourced can be planted in great numbers, harvested and then replanted. Tencel, Modal and Lenpur are all sourced from treebark. While viscose can be produced from all sorts of raw materials, the most successful alternative to beech trees at the moment is bamboo, which has been planted in Northern Italy among other places specifically to service the textile industry. Bamboo is one of the fastest growing plants and thus an easily renewable resource. The processing of viscose, however, uses chemicals to dissolve the wood fibres. Massive resources have been devoted to refining methods of production to minimise damage to the environment.

A notable player is Lenzing, the Austrian firm that produces Tencel, the research-rich company which has developed totally closed production cycles for its viscose, meaning that the water and chemicals used for manufacturing the fibre are continually cleaned and then reused during production.

The remarkable properties of wood provide textile materials with extraordinary attributes that reflect its original source. Viscose is great at moisture absorption and temperature regulation plus it also has deodorant qualities. The fabric is also soft with a graceful flow. It feels like cotton, and also has the advantages of shiny silk.

Crab shells and crustacea are the latest elements to be used with viscose. Lenzing's new Tencel®C fabrics and Pozzi Electa's Crabyon® fabrics are produced from discarded crab shells blended with viscose and are used particularly for soft and fine underwear, for they possess natural anti-bacterial qualities, reducing odour and bacteria in sweat.

Ingeo™ fibre is made from one of the most available

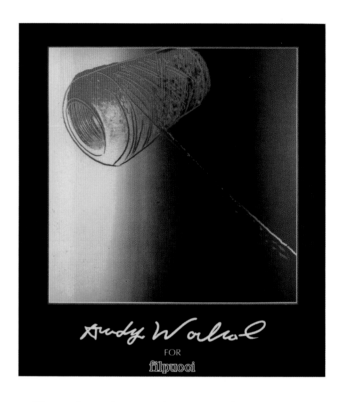

© *The acclaimed Rocca Fantasia by Andy Warhol for the 1983 Filpucci advertising campaign*
Filpucci yarn is a mythmaker as far as fashion is concerned. In the 1960s Andy Warhol famously drew this rather delicate view of the magic of yarn. Design and invention have been at the forefront of the firm's drivers, and the name Filpucci is one of the aristocracy of the Italian textile trade, which is itself composed of a glittering panoply of family tradition, film, glamour and a certain intellectualism.

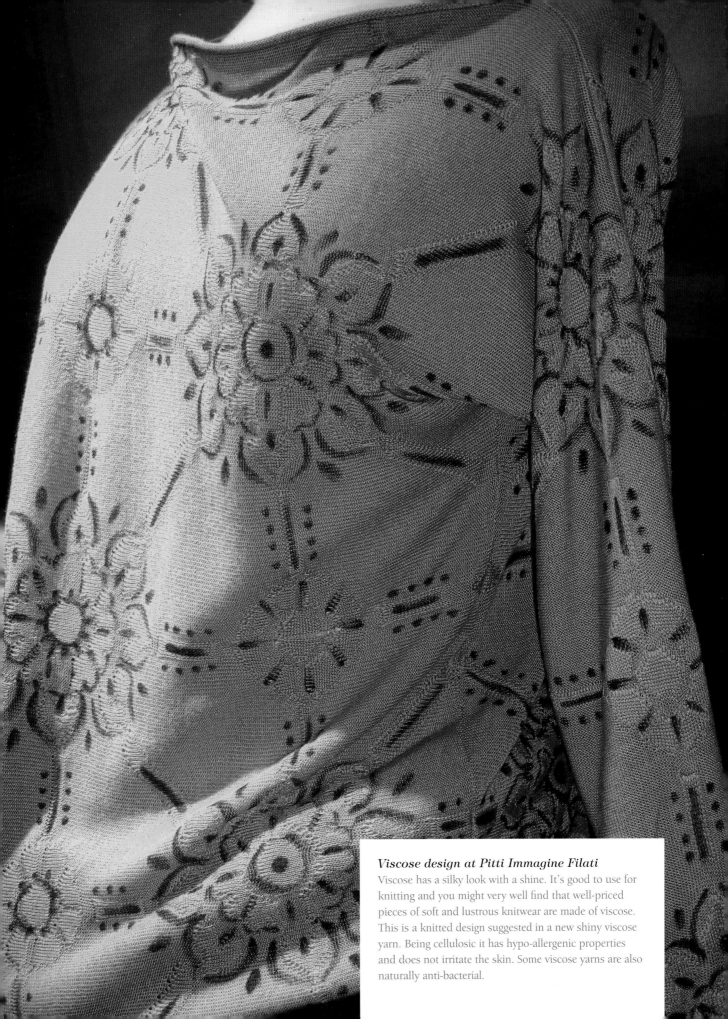

Viscose design at Pitti Immagine Filati

Viscose has a silky look with a shine. It's good to use for knitting and you might very well find that well-priced pieces of soft and lustrous knitwear are made of viscose. This is a knitted design suggested in a new shiny viscose yarn. Being cellulosic it has hypo-allergenic properties and does not irritate the skin. Some viscose yarns are also naturally anti-bacterial.

sources: corn fibre from maize. It claims to be the first fibre to be synthesized from an annually renewable resource. By fermenting corn sugar into lactic acid, which in turn is converted to polylactic acid resin, the resin is then spun into fibre. Ingeo™ has properties similar to petroleum-based synthetic fibres, but maize fibre does not contribute to greenhouse gases and is totally biodegradable. One drawback is that it is now competing with the bio-fuels market geared towards the automotive industry.

Coffee, milk and sugar can now be worn. This seems an odd statement, but viscose-type textiles can be made from the most surprising materials. There are fabrics being created from stinging nettles, milk solids, coffee grounds, soya, and plant matter which is heated into a type of sugar. It's an example of recycling and renewal that has become a reality.

Viscose blends

Viscose is found in fashion collections from formal to casual. It's often mixed with luxury precious fibres to create fabric with a more approachable price point, for example mixed with cashmere it can feel more comforting or with Lurex® it gains a touch of glitter. It's used for shirts, skirts, summer jackets and dresses, mixed with cotton and wools. With its characteristic softness and drape, viscose is nice to wear. Knitted into jersey it is found in all sorts of designs from flirty skirts to slinky sheath dresses.

Pitti Immagine Filati

Pitti Immagine Filati is the big Italian yarn show which, along with Expofil in Paris and Filo Yarns in Milan, attracts buyers and designers who want to know what's brewing up in the fashion world in terms of colour, special fabrics and ingredients for the mix. It's where the ideas start to come to the surface, to be picked up and interpreted in many different ways. It's the reason why, when the new season's clothes come into the fashion stores, there is a remarkable thread of colour, shape and design that runs through them. It all starts there at the beginning of the supply chain.

"Green" T-shirts

Young fashion brands want to do things their own way. This often involves an eco approach to their whole trading philosophy; how the garments are made, and particularly what fabrics are selected. Here is one of a series of T-shirts in 'green' fabrics such as viscose. Rapanui Clothing is made in a factory using solar and wind power and is committed to ethical fashion. The complete package, explained on their website gives detailed information about their ethics and reasons for using fabrics such as viscose and organic cotton.

Fashion made from milk

Outsider is an up and coming, eco-focused company run by talented London designer, Noorin Khamisani, who makes coveted, smart clothing from natural eco-friendly fabrics such as viscose, silk and cotton. This dress shows how fabrics can look a million dollars, while still retaining the benefits of sustainable production. Outsider's use of viscose, including milk viscose, silk, cotton and other 'green' fabrics in a stylish way, gives a trendy image to eco fabrics sought out by younger fashion followers.

She sells sea shells

The benefits of viscose-type fabrics are well known, trumped by Lenzing's latest invention Tencel®C. This is made of chitin, a biopolymer extracted from seashells and crab shells. Lenzing make this on a large scale. Tencel® and Chitosan are complementary as they're both natural products, one derived from beech trees, the other from shrimps, prawns and crabs, and there are millions of kilos of these around. Chitosan is already used in cosmetics and pharmaceuticals to alleviate itchiness, protect the skin and it has antibacterial properties. The Chitosan is taken out of the shells and applied to the Tencel® fibre and cosmetic benefits last during washing. Tests show that it acts as a moisture reservoir, limiting dehydration and moisture loss, and accelerating cell renewal during wound healing.

Italian viscose made from seashells is appealingly called Crabyon®. Crabyon® also has proven anti-bacterial qualities so it's ideal for use in bodywear and lingerie as well as babywear, where it has a particular appeal. As does German fibre Sea-Cell®.

3

Synthetic and high-tech fabrics

Synthetic and high-tech fabrics

What is a micro-climate?

HIGH-TECH fabrics are an expanding area. While we may primarily encounter them in stores specialising sports or hiking and camping, where cagoules, trousers, shorts, T-shirts and fleeces have explanatory leaflets to accompany them, high-tech elements are also finding their way into mainstream clothing.

Polyester, which is petrochemical based, is the biggest selling fibre in the world, with over 70% of the world's market. Everyone knows polyester, which became popular in the 20th century because it was easy care and priced lower price than many other fabrics, but now high-quality polyester yarn with special powers and advantages is often incorporated into high-tech developments.

Scientists and fabric technologists have invested huge amounts of money into research on improving the performance of garments. This means that clothing is designed not only to be attractive and comfortable, but also to have additional attributes that protect against the elements.

Fibres have been developed for fabrics said to prevent harmful emissions from mobile phones and other electronic gadgets buzzing around in the atmosphere. One such fabric can be used to line pockets where you put your phone and shield your body from any emissions. Advances such as black

In textile terms it means creating a capsule-like protection for the body, maintaining a comfortable temperature, even in extreme heat or biting cold, keeping wind and rain outside by transferring warmth and moisture where it's needed.

Nylon yarn with essential shine

Synthetic is often an unpopular fibre, but it is supremely important in the fashion trade and even in top designers' collections. Polyester, polyamide, nylon and acrylic are often blended with natural fibres for extra strength, for effects like shine and sparkle and for stretch, the all-important feature. New synthetics can be soft, fine and there are microfibre versions of them. All are easy care. In addition, the most advanced developments and scientific solutions have been in synthetic technology, addressing the problems of protective and active clothing. And as performance features are put into fashion garments such as macs, coats and jackets, there's a greater emphasis on colour and design.

fabrics that stay cool in high temperatures, or layers of clothing that can sense the ambient temperature and react, preventing chafing and friction, are widely welcomed.

At the cutting edge, scientists are working on fabrics that contain sensors to monitor the wearer's vital signs. Such fabrics could be useful in war zones, to assess heart attack victims or to diagnose the condition of people trapped somewhere.

Skiwear, professional and amateur cycling fabrics, clothing for athletics and swimming have all been the focus of high-tech, highly resourced companies in Europe, Japan, US and South Korea, resulting in the creation of lightweight, body-hugging and practical comfort fabrics. When used in professional swimming and athletics, these aerodynamic garments can trim seconds off race times.

High-tech nylon, polyamide and polyester fabrics used in combination with other yarns and fibres, provide highly complex wicking layers, using mesh, coatings and constructions, which move sweat to the outside of the garment and keep the elements out. Further sophistication has led to optimising the effectiveness of layering, which means that base layers, mid layers and outer layers work together to reduce discomfort, wetness, abrasion or sweaty heat. Nano-sized particles are often involved in coating fabrics for optimum effect.

One example is the use of nylon or polyamide shells on the outside and down fillings or wafer-thin membranes inside. These are engineered to prevent moisture getting in (rain or snow) while still allowing it to get out (sweat and steam) by means of the size of the holes in the fabric. Gore-Tex®,

Outlast®, Coolmax® are all fabric technologies which control the body's microclimate in various ways, protecting the wearer regardless of the weather or the activities he or she may be involved in.

Many inventions have taken their cue from nature. Schoeller, an immensely creative company invented c_change™ technology, research inspired by the example of a fir cone opening and closing in response to different weather conditions.

Developments originally focussed on athletics and sports are being adopted by high-end fashion designers. Cycling and skiing have inspired inventions to make fabrics light, comfortable and able to perform in extreme conditions, and they are available for fashion garments too. Urban cycling has prompted the use of 'professional' fabrics for clothes which can equally well be worn into the office. Cool Italian labels like Zegna, Giorgio Armani or Loro Piana use special coatings, membranes and liners to add microclimate technology to wool jackets and mixed fibre urban wear.

Performance factors are not confined to synthetics. Many natural fabrics are having their advantages re-assessed. Wool has natural water repellent properties and climate control capabilities, among other factors. Cotton, woven tightly, can be coated, lacquered, rubberised or waxed for protection, like Barbour jackets. Linen is a dynamic fashion fabric; now techno coatings and finishes extend its powers. And companies such as Nano-tex are using nanotechnology on natural fabrics to make them stain and wrinkle resistant.

High-tech polyester fibre

Outlast® is widely used in fabrics for thermo-regulation. The company's motte is 'not too hot, not too cold, just right' – the 'Goldilocks and the Three Bears' approach. The technology developed out of research by NASA for the space programme. Phase Change Materials, or PCMs, absorb excess heat from the body, store it in microcapsules in the fabric and when you start to cool down, release the heat back to the body, keeping the microclimate comfortable. It's also widely used in footwear such as sports shoes and fashion boots.

Technical fabrics for running and leisure wear

Technical fabrics that produce a microclimate, protect the body against extremes of heat and cold, using insulation, wicking sweat away from the body and preventing the wet penetrating the garment from the outside, often by use of a technical membrane with various sizes of pores or holes. Gore-Tex® is the most well known waterproof/breathable fabric. It is laminated to high performance textiles and then seam-sealed for waterproof protection. You'll find it in most places where people are involved in professional sports, leisure pursuits like walking, hiking or mountaineering, and on high streets and shopping malls across the world.

Polyester techno-fashion with YKK Vision ® zipper

Accessories for high performing garments need technical zippers and fastenings too. Most of these are made from synthetic fibres. Here is a polyester zipper in a bright neon colour; colour is a major feature of skiwear, jackets and activewear. YKK, incidentally, make more than 90% of all the zippers in the world, including diamond encrusted couture versions, and even fastenings made from fire-resistant materials.

The fashion for cycling

Cycling has become a sexy sport, with sales of wonder bikes and stylish high-tech clothing increasing worldwide for sporty amateurs. Eschler is renowned for technically developed, functional textiles that have comfort as a major factor. Cycling has seen a huge growth in interest among the public. Once confined to the riders in the Tour de France, the 21st-century Olympic Games have cemented its popularity among spectators all over the world. As a result, cycling is the fastest growing amateur sport in many countries, with streamlined performance clothes an essential ingredient in the mix. The number of people cycling to work has also increased in all the capitals of the world, many using high performance comfort clothes before changing at the office.

Fabrics designed for cycling are now highly complex and technical. Compression and aerodynamics are key areas of design; compression to improve blood flow in the extremities and reducing the production of lactic acid in the body, which can slow the rider down. Polyester and elastane (stretch fibre) are used for these energy saving and thermo-regulating fabrics. Protection against UV rays, which can cause cancers, is also built into these fabrics also found widely in T-shirts and casual wear. It'll be on the label.

Note: In the 2012 Summer Olympics, British medal winners, including Chris Hoy, were described as wearing revolutionary 'hot pants' in fabric with heated strips to keep the leg muscles warm between events in order to increase sprint power. It highlights the close links between the textile industry and research institutions and universities across the world. Universities and research institutes are particularly strong in the Far East, China, and South Korea because research on textiles can pay dividends and make scientific reputations. In this case of hot pants, it was co-operation between Loughborough University in England, Adidas and British Cycling. The idea is compared to tire warmers in Formula 1!

Techno fabric for active fashion sportswear

Metals play a part in technology for textiles as techniques become more sophisticated. The great innovators in techno textiles not only make fabrics for serious athletes, but also for the fashion market. The latest mixes such as lightweight cotton/polyamide/polyester have glow-in-the-dark coatings or fine threads of irregular copper wire which are used in a very light collection of Schoeller®-Spirit fabrics. Metal used in designs make the fabrics shimmer and move, while aluminium foil coatings on transparent gauze play with light and shade. Steel fibres make it possible to bend the fabric into particular shapes. Silver additives for fabrics have proven anti-microbial effects that neutralise the bacteria built up in sweat, reduce the risk of infections (in medical textiles) and prevent odours. Anti-odour silver is, unsurprisingly, used extensively for the best quality men's socks. Silver is appearing more frequently in bodywear, activewear and lingerie. The latest versions include silver encapsulated in glass ceramic material so that the clothes can be washed frequently without affecting the benefits.

Fabrics push at the boundaries of science

The textile technologists are always pushing the boundaries to solve intractable problems, to enhance and transform fabrics. Stone Island, the Italian cult fashion label, has a reputation for innovation and experimentation, including mixing natural and super technical fibres in fashion garments. An exhibition in Florence exhibited its ground-breaking techno fashions over the years, including this jacket with Kevlar. Kevlar is a protective fibre that is stronger than steel, and because of its high tensile strength has been used in body armour among other things.

Among the latest developments are cosmetic fabrics, which incorporate substances such as aloe vera or other moisturisers or anti-aging creams that are then gradually released by thousands of microcapsules in the yarn as the fabric moves. This is causing much excitement in beauty circles and is still a work-in-progress.

How to make black fabrics reflect rather than absorb heat is something textile technologists have been working on for years; white is popular in hot countries primarily because it reflects heat away from you. Ermenegildo Zegna, the Italian fashion house, has introduced its Cool Effect fabric innovation for its stylish collections in fine Merino wool with a special finish said to render the fabric's temperature ten degrees lower in the sun than untreated fabrics. Coldblack® by Schoeller is a revolutionary finish which can be used on dark and black fabrics of all sorts, reflecting the heat back, and has hit the press headlines including The New York Times. It also provides factor 30 UV protection from the sun's rays.

Nanotechnology, the buzz science of today, is heavily involved in textile developments. Teflon finishes on suiting fabrics make wool clothes resistant to stains, and Schoeller have developed NanoSphere ® which makes fabrics self-cleaning, dirt and liquid simply roll off the fabrics, preventing stains. This is only the beginning of the relationship between nanoscience and textiles.

Fabrics with a memory

Fabrics with a shape memory combine fashion and function, for example polyester with a high proportion of elastic fibre or combined with other synthetics. Schoeller's techno fabrics are made with natural fibres such as cotton or wool as well as with high-tech yarns, using modern coating and finishing technologies for stunning fashion effects. Here you can seeSchoeller®-styltec 25% stretch polyurethane, 77% polyester.

Invista, who own the Lycra® fibre brand, in partnership with sportswear brand Fila, have developed a body toning system with double layers of Lycra® Sport fabric for women, using stretch fibre technology. This is claimed to increase muscle exercise by as much as 50%. The fact that it says it can compress the muscles and smooth target areas to reduce the appearance of cellulite might very well be a winner.

Performance fabrics for golfing and fashion

Coolmax® is one of the leading performance fabrics which include moisture management as part of the system. It is made from polyester specially engineered to have an increased surface area with four or six channels that pull moisture away from the skin to the outer layer of fabric so that it can dry quickly. Like many of the fabrics in this high-tech section, it was developed for athletes but is so versatile that it is used in many other areas of fashion; sportswear, ready-to-wear and bodywear. It's used widely for sports like cycling and golfing, but it also is appearing in high performance fashion. Inventive young brand Hot Squash uses easy-care Coolmax® polyester for its elegant, flowing clothes.

Serious technical clothing for the outdoors

Only for those with a sense of style. Seriously technical outdoor clothing like this range by Canadian specialists Arc'teryx, have a huge following of devotees, and include fleeces, soft shells and snow sport gear to protect you from the elements. Fabrics used for these garments are layered within each jacket to regulate the microclimate and keep you comfortable. The first layer is for quick moisture transport and optimum thermo regulation, the second layer is for insulation and the outer layer is for wind and weather protection. Good elasticity is crucial, because the garments have to be quite tight yet offer maximum freedom of movement.

Tweed meets techno

This fleeing fellow wearing a tweed coat by Dashing Tweeds which has 3M reflective yarns incorporated into the weave. It was created by Russell Howarth at Graham Browne.3M make most of the high quality reflective tape used on work wear, sportswear and reflective safety items, their reflective yarn called Retroglo® is composed of tiny glass prisms. Dashing Tweeds developed their tweed fabric using this reflective yarn, and called it Lumatwill™. It's an example of the fashion trend to bring the country into a metropolitan setting, using fancy wool weaves for coats and jackets that look smart enough for wearing in a capital city, and have that extra touch of urban chic. This is a trend that has been seen in many designer collections as a way of creating traditional quality with an ultra techno twist.

Dress to light up the night

High-tech developments are not confined to sportswear. This is one of the more spectacular high-tech fabric areas, more or less opened up by CuteCircuit, a London-based company founded by two designers, Ryan Genz and Francesca Rosella.

They have developed smart textiles and microelectronics and have wowed the celebrity world by producing dresses covered with LED lights, which have appeared on stage worn by such stars as Katy Perry and in major fashion shows. One of CuteCircuit's dazzling illuminated electronic dresses has been selected as part of the permanent collection of the Museum of Science and Industry in Chicago.

The company's spectacular designs are available to the public and have been sold in fashion stores like Selfridges. In their prêt-à-porter collection, designs use 3D digital prints and Bluetooth devices. The designers have also created the M dress with a SIM card to make and receive phone calls without a phone. This idea has also been incorporated into some menswear designs by suit manufacturers, notably in India.

Electronics woven into fabrics is an ongoing area of research, and textile technologists are developing fabrics that can monitor health, blood pressure, and the oxygen content of the blood. The system can also monitor exercise and its effects for fitness addicts.

Textile keyboards, wireless Bluetooth systems allowing music to play from a pocket straight to a receiver in the ear; phone calls which can be made by a gesture of the hand, are a result of sophisticated communication and internet devices which can be incorporated into all types of clothing. It's an area of dynamic research. Some clothing with electronic circuits incorporated can be washed and the battery problem is addressed by solar cells, with limited success so far, it must be said.

A parallel idea is that of lining pockets with anti-electronic fabrics to prevent radiation from devices and phones from touching the body. However, because this is now perceived as less of a threat, there is apparently less interest in the development, but research continues in all these areas.

4

Eco fabrics and sustainability

Eco fabrics and sustainability

How can your clothes protect you from harm?

The eco movement seeks to minimise harmful chemicals, emissions and damage to the environment using green, natural advantages for protection

Eco clothes and textiles are increasingly popular but it can be confusing, because the term eco covers a number of worthy attitudes. Basically it means that fabrics are ecologically sound, or green, in terms of their impact on the environment and use of sustainable practices in their manufacture.

Organic fabrics are made to much stricter standards, certified with a guarantee that fabrics and clothing are monitored as being free of contaminants and that the fabrics can be traced from the farm to the store. There are several of these certifications all of which differ slightly, but they all guarantee a level of quality and care for the way fabrics are made.

Sustainability means being sparing with natural resources and using renewable raw materials where possible, replanting, regrowing, reusing waste products and above all reducing the carbon footprint.

The green approach to fashion

One of the most exciting developments in textiles is the eco movement, the green approach to fashion. It's acknowledged that heavy industry and chemical activities have damaged the environment and been a major source of air and water pollution. Textiles have been implicated in this over the past two centuries. But now the textile industry has recognised the need to incorporate sustainable and ecologically sound practices into their production. There is a move, therefore, towards attaining zero emissions and low carbon and CO_2 build-up in the environment, and this has become a source of pride to many companies.

Concern about environmental impact is not just confined to the fringe, but is becoming mainstream. Textile companies, including large manufacturers in China, are investigating recycling wastewater, natural plant-based dyestuffs and using biodegradable materials. Large companies like Marks & Spencer, leaders in this area, have produced detailed corporate policies on emissions, stressing sustainability. There is also a heartening growth of small craft companies producing handmade textiles, reviving ancient crafts and promoting 'slow fashion'. This echoes the move in 'slow food,' that is to go back to the principles of good natural ingredients and ways of doing things.

The eco movement and concerns about the environment have made a big impact on the fashion trade and consumers. It's made people think about how and where things are made, how much they affect the people who make them, the way raw materials are obtained, and the conditions under which textiles are produced. It forces people to question whether the vast industry which is fashion can be an ethical and sustainable one, and it's leading to some very exciting and imaginative solutions on a small and large scale.

The discovery, or rediscovery, of organic fabrics and recycling yarns, fabrics and clothing has been a revelation to a whole new generation who weren't around in the 1960s, where it all started. This time it's entered into the wider consciousness.

The emphasis is on using what is natural, minimisingchemicals and reusing perfectly good clothes. It has affected the large-scale producers of synthetic fabrics too, who are refining their methods and husbanding their resources, stressing responsible production.

Parents have begun to look at the fabrics they will dress their babies in, seeking out the purest, softest and least intrusive. So-called healthy fabrics can be a reality with testing and labelling plus the added benefit of lessening pollution. Official labels such as Oeko-Tex®, an international testing and accreditation system for screening textiles, prove that the fabrics comply with certain ecological standards. The Soil Association also certifies to the Global Organic Textile Standards (GOTS) – the international gold standard for organic textiles. The whole supply chain from field through manufacture to final product must be certified, checked against both environmental and social standards.

Silver fibres are used medically and now have been introduced into sportswear to reduce bacteria growth, fewer insecticides on crops, harsh chemicals in dyeing and finishing, and processes like the recirculation and reuse of water necessary for spinning, weaving and dyeing benefit the whole environment. It looks like win-win.

Save our Seas Rapanui bamboo viscose T-shirt

Designer Katharine Hamnett was the queen of the right-on slogan 20 years ago. New designer/activists for the environment like Rapanui, committed to eco principles, use natural fabrics to proclaim green slogans to a similarly engaged customer. The growth of interest in the environment has also led to a revival in vintage and second hand clothing, up-cycling, and recycling, the reuse of clothes and refashioning of existing materials is taking place on an individual and an industrial scale.

Three eco fabrics: silk, cotton and bamboo, all dyed with natural plant based dyes

Silk, cotton and bamboo are all classed as eco fabrics, because they are natural in origin and, in this case, dyed with natural plants. Italian company Tintoria di Quaregna has led the field in developing dyes which are not only natural, but are also, in their complexity and range of vibrant colours, accepted by mainstream fabric manufacturers as reliable and repeatable.

Over thirty types of natural dyes derived from sandalwood, henna, blackberry, turmeric, tansy and lately indigo are on offer, and generally taken up by the very top end of the industry, where eco credentials are highly sought after.

Trendy knitted top in pure linen

Acne Studios is a directional Swedish fashion company which uses a lot of natural fibres. It prides itself on its spare, modern lines, and natural fibres fit the profile. Choosing natural fibres can be a fashion statement in itself. Linen fabric, has very good eco credentials, and is associated with 'cool' designers who like working with it because of its mix of sophistication and authentic green image.

High fashion eco fabric

An Italian company with excellent eco credentials, Taiana shows that eco fabrics can have a high fashion content, being chosen for many well-known brands. Taiana makes fabrics for both women and men, including shirtings and fabrics from recycled yarn.

Natural Dyes from Tintoria di Quaregna

Dyeing has been a source of pollution and negative effects on the environment since the large-scale manufacture of cloth began in the 1790s. Powerful dyestuffs were being used that subsequently drained off into rivers and, when not controlled, caused substantial damage to wildlife, their habitat and sometimes to the surrounding human population. Some of these dyes are now banned.

Nowadays people are much more concerned about the effects of manufacturing processes on the environment, and improvements have been backed up by legislation, which, although it varies from country to country, has spurred many enterprises to limit the potentially harmful effects their business might have. As a result, the responsible areas of the textile trade aim for almost zero emissions or waste products to taint the environment, for example in Yorkshire, where local rivers next to the mills used to run with the colour of the cloth, not so long ago.

Tintoria di Quaregna, the Italian dyer and finisher, is one of the pioneers in producing commercially viable, natural dyes for fashion yarns as well as using conventional dyeing techniques and ingredients. Below is their latest list of natural dyes.

See how many herb names you recognise. They include nuts, barks and berries for various shades of brown; horsetail, onions, logwood and acacia. Greens from leaves, pinks and reds from such plants as madder and cochineal, dark greys and blacks from roots like liquorice and juniper, blue from indigo plants, bright yellow and orange from ground-up powders like turmeric and sandalwood. Each season the list grows longer, an essential part of the organic and eco chain which accentuates the natural in what we wear. Many of these tinctures and powders have been known for centuries, a comforting thought in many ways.

Here are the English names and the botanical names in Latin.

English name	Botanical name
Dyer's Bugloss	*Alkanna Tinctoria*
Logwood Tree	*Haematoxylum Campechianum*
Chestnut	*Castanea Sativa*
Cutch tree (Acacia)	*Acacia Catechu*
Onion	*Allium Cepa*
Cochineal	*Coccus Cacti*
Common Barberry	*Berberis Vulgari*
Ivy	*Hedera Helix*
Horsetail	*Equisetum Arvense*
Alder Buckthorn	*Rhamnus Alnus*
Juniper	*Juniperis Communis*
Egyptian Privet	*Lawsonia inermis*
Indigo plant	*Indigofera Tinctoria*
Liquorice	*Glycyrrhiza Glabra*
Pomegranate	*Punica Granatum*
Blueberry	*Vaccinium Myrtillus*
Black Walnut	*Juglans regia*
Poppy	*Papaver Rhoeas*
Rhubarb	*Rheum Officinalis*
Weld	*Reseda Luteola*
Madder	*Rubia Tinctorum*
Curled Dock	*Rumex Crispus*
Red Sandalwood	*Pterocarpus Santelinus*
Black Tea	*Camellia Thea*

Miroglio's NewLife® yarn in fabric by Frizza

Italy has been a leader in green approaches, and fabric companies have been experimenting with weaving new yarns. The slow food movement has gradually found an echo with 'slow' fashion being seen as important in reducing harmful substances and even promoting health and wellbeing. Regeneration or recycling is a prime example of this 'waste not, want not' attitude.

Prato, the textile area near Florence, has specialised in recycling for centuries. It has recently found a new appetite for it, and the town is officially producing regenerated, carbon neutral fabrics made with recycled wool, with zero emissions.

Miroglio fabric made from NewLife®

One of the most successful recycling stories is NewLife®. It's polyester filament made from plastic water bottles. These used bottles are collected on an organised scale in northern Italy, washed, treated, then heated and spun into new yarn which can be woven into fabrics, usually destined for the top end of fashion. The amount of chemicals involved are minimal.

Another recycling development is the recycling of cotton or woollen yarn, either from off-cuts collected when garments are cut out in the factories, or by collecting old clothing, taking it apart, capturing the fibre and spinning it into something totally new. The fibres can be used in the colours of the original yarn or dyed into completely new colours.

Ethical practices

This garment is a happy coincidence of endangered species and bamboo fabric, which makes up the panda's diet in China. Animals feature heavily in the eco movement and organic standards include the welfare of animals. This sometimes involves the banning of mulesing (docking the tails of lambs to prevent fly-strike) although opinions on this practice, if humanely carried out, are varied since fly-strike is a menace which causes much suffering in large flocks of sheep in Australia, New Zealand and elsewhere. These debates and concerns go alongside the banning of dangerous chemicals in some manufacturing, campaigned about by Greenpeace, and finding a platform for ecological concerns.

OPPOSITE, TOP *Young designers change direction*
Many young and hip labels are associated with the green movement; this is particularly true of Outsider whose founder, Noorin Khamisani, has built her design business totally on eco principles. Ethical practices and eco fabrics are typical of the attitude of committed eco designers springing up in Britain, Holland, Germany, and the US particularly. Across the globe, younger people believe that wearing eco-friendly clothes chimes with their world view.

OPPOSITE, RIGHT *Organic cotton, eco fabrics and ethical fashion – spot the difference?*
Organic and eco cotton looks exactly the same as conventional cotton. Here is a slightly chintzy look in organic cotton, coloured coffee and cream.

More and more fashion business takes place on the internet, reaching out to an international audience. Descriptions and information about what fabrics are made of is a must for successful internet trading. You'll find that ethical fashion and organic fabrics are better explained than most 'ordinary' websites.

NewLife® recycled yarn

None of the glamorous creations that have been seen on carpets, either red or green, has had as much impact as seeing Livia Firth and Meryl Streep wearing eco dresses by Giorgio Armani and Lanvin respectively. Penelope Cruz wore a vintage Balmain to the Oscars. Fabrics like this brilliant blue by Miroglio show there's nothing dowdy about recycling and eco fabrics, appealing across the board to stylish fashion wearers.

Silky recycled polyester This printed polyester dress fabric appeared in directional fabric on show at French international exhibition, Premiere Vision. It's another example of the way that environmentally sound and recycled fabrics can be used in exactly the same way as conventional textiles. This example from Miroglio by Tessitura Virgilio Taiana.

***Naturetec by Schoeller, combining natural fibres,
technology and bluesign® sustainability***

This fabric is a soft-shell in soft brushed wool, with the wool on
the inside and nylon on the outside. It is machine washable and
conforms with bluesign® standards. The wool used is from South
America.

Companies who make sportswear for active people find that
customers who spend a lot of time outdoors tend to be ecologically
minded and demand information about how their clothing is
made. Bluesign is another certification for manufacturers of
textiles, which produces tools for sustainable practices covering
raw materials to dyers and manufacturers through to retailers.
Sustainable manufacturing, reducing emissions, reusing water
and recycling materials has gained impetus from the philosophy
of mainly younger fashion designers and new, hip labels. It has
spread internationally throughout the industry on a massive scale.

Sustainability: recycling and regeneration

On the face of it recycled fabric from used clothing sounds a bit dodgy – as does fabric from used plastic water bottles. But this is actually an exciting part of the responsible and sustainable production to which much of the forward-thinking fashion trade has signed up. The most exquisite fabrics can be created by the recycling industry, which can produce polyester yarn from used water bottles, cotton from recycled denim, new wool from old jumpers. It's cool to be green.

There are two main methods of recycling. In the first, new, coloured yarn comes from factory off-cuts left over when patterns are cut from fabric. These used to be thrown away or used for rags. Now they are all carefully collected, washed, processed, unravelled and spun into new fibre. The second method recycles cotton, polyester, or wool, by stripping it out of existing old garments and creating a completely new fabric that can be dyed and used again.

The Italian firm Miroglio has hit the jackpot on the current trend for cool recycling by fashioning new polyester yarn from used water bottles. To make one kilogram of Newlife™ yarn, it takes 31.5 one-litre plastic bottles.

The glamorous eco warrior Livia Firth, wife of actor Colin Firth, invented the 'green carpet' named to rival the red version. She galvanised the fashion world with an elegant appearance at the Golden Globes in 2012 in a Giorgio Armani dress made from recycled polyester entirely from Newlife™. Meryl Streep then accepted her Oscar for Best Actress wearing a golden Lanvin dress from eco fabric, and the fashion's green movement was on its way. 'Upcycling', making garments of top quality off-cuts and well-designed eco fabrics, makes the whole concept desirable.

How can worn-out jeans be resurrected for a second life?
They can be washed, unravelled and respun into new cotton and start a life as something completely different.

What does recycled polyester start life as?
The best-known recycled polyester started life as plastic water bottles, collected in their thousands from special bins in northern Italy.

Oeko-Tex® yarn – an important standard for fabrics
This standard certifies the absence of harmful substances, and is widely adopted throughout the world, including the many different manufacturing environments growing exponentially in China and the Far East. As surveys reveal, people throughout the supply chain recognise these standards as being of growing importance to their customers.

All along the way, the environmental impact of textile-making is being reduced and the steps need to be traceable. In other words, the life of the textile from fibre to fashion is documented. So traceability accounts for all the steps and journeys raw materials, fibres, yarns and fabrics make before they are bought as a garment. Degradable textiles and reusable elements are key to this, dubbed a cradle-to-cradle policy. All this is very important to the many consumers who are environmentally aware.

The scope for materials that can be recycled or dismantled and reborn is growing in sophistication and appeal. Designer brands and powerful retailers are developing new ideas to capture the customers' imagination. Marks & Spencer has introduced 'shwopping' where customers are encouraged to bring in an unwanted piece of clothing for recycling every time they buy something new.

Students and designers have been inspired to research and eventually relocate designer clothes; beautiful silks, wools and cottons found among the dross in second-hand shops. It's leading to a way of life that has influenced today's emphasis on heritage. The green approach is finding popularity on an international scale.

Schwopping, Marks & Spencer's bright idea, swap something old when you buy something new

Most large international companies have produced plans to improve the sustainability of their operations. Shareholders expect it, with a section in the Annual Report. Big fashion retailers such as H&M have also introduced eco-friendly policies, almost out-doing each other with their ambitious plans. H&M has also recognised the importance of cooperation, stressing that the industry must act together to achieve zero discharge. Marks & Spencer have had a sophisticated Plan A in place for several years (There is no Plan B) and want to be the most sustainable high street retailer in only a few years' time.

Water management and chemical use is monitored from small mills to large industrial complexes, in response to the world view and individual lobbying.

Systema Naturae

Cariaggi, the cashmere specialist, has a deep commitment to green issues and produces ecological collections. The colours are sourced from medicinal herbs, leaves, berries and roots, including Guado, or woad, under the name Systema Naturae, the result of research carried out with Italian universities to dye cashmere with environmentally friendly elements. The colours are unique, recalling Italian tapestries.

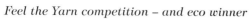

Feel the Yarn competition – and eco winner

Young designers setting up in business, and those still studying at colleges are notably enthused by sustainable fashion. Feel the Yarn is the annual competition held in Florence to identify the most innovative designs by students in top art colleges across the world. It was won in 2012 by Li Xiao from the Royal College of Art, with an ingenious painted garment which featured eco and recycled yarns by Pinori Filati.

If you want to find fashionable high-quality garments, try and seek out young designers bursting with ideas. Go to the end of term graduate shows, where the garments are often for sale, attend exhibitions and craft fairs, look on the web, patronise the young designers, because they are usually working on clothes that will last.

5
Heritage fabrics

Heritage fabrics

THE HERITAGE movement is gathering momentum in the 21st century and inspiring people to re-examine and redis-cover things that are in danger of being lost in many cultures. It is about preserving skills and traditions and in textiles there is still a lot to retrieve and cherish. The value of heritage is central to today's wish to take the past and recast it for mod-ern times. It is driving designers and stylists to look in vintage shops, study photographs and, above all, to take inspiration from the still extant and meticulously kept archives of mills, textile companies and merchants which can yield up treasures.

Secondhand shops are a treasure trove for people who are looking for design and individuality or seeking out new and original handmade clothing. People have realised that there is a lot to rediscover in fashion that is built to last. Not only does this type of clothing mark out individuality, but it also is a way of spending money more carefully by building on what was good from the past.

Designers are looking to their heritage to re-interpret the best in a new way. As a result, heritage fabrics are being made in lighter weights and with a much softer feel than the uncom-promising originals to suit modern life. Traditional designs were often taken from the natural world, and techniques like digital printing have revived these inspirations, but designers might choose to reinterpret these designs in different colours.

Sturdy sporting cloths like Cheviots from the Scottish borders, colourful tweeds, German felted lodens, Italian and French silks, Swiss fine cottons, as well as country fabrics like corduroys and tweeds are staging a comeback in fashion with people of all ages, especially if they live in the big city.

If a design has a name and a story, we are even more interested. It's all part of the modern quest for heritage and tra-ditional values which is affecting all our lives.

The inspirational landscape of the Scottish Isles

Hebridean yarn

The majority of heritage fabrics are deeply embedded in the surroundings where they originated. Tweeds reflect the tones of the hedgerows and flowers, greens and browns with flashes of sun. Harris Tweed in particular has always made the link between the fabric and the landscape, something which has been understood by customers around the world. Todd & Duncan, the cashmere spinners, draw on their Scottish surroundings for inspiration for their colour palettes.

The orb mark

The popularity of Harris Tweed, still woven in the traditional way by law, has gathered momentum recently, coinciding with the passion for revisiting our history. The Harris Tweed brand is being steered by people who have recognised that the only way to retain a unique way of life is by striking a chord with modern tastes. With an emphasis on lighter weights, softer qualities and a feeling for the mood of the moment, Harris Tweed is still traditionally produced, and every length has to carry the orb mark to show that it has been handloomed on the Island of Harris.

The popularity of tweed

The former image of a dotty old lady in thick, scratchy tweeds has been split apart by images such as this one. Harris Tweed has proved that customers like to reference the past and to recast it in each generation. The time-travelling TV hero Dr Who's Harris Tweed jacket became the 'must have' garment after the recent series, and accounted for an unprecedented raid on Oxfam and thrift shops by visitors to the UK, as well as by the residents, to hunt down the last of the 'real' Harris Tweed. By popular demand, the sturdy fabric is lighter and softer than it was, but it still acts as a shield against most weather, and retains its connection to the landscape.

Tweed has regained an enormous following overseas, particularly in fashion-conscious Japan and France. It has been used by Paul Smith, Vivienne Westwood, Calvin Klein, Ralph Lauren, and even on trendy sneakers by Nike, for which weaver Donald John Mackay was made an MBE (an honour awarded by the Queen) and recently on Clarks shoes.

Harris Tweed also contributed to a hike in export sales of all sorts of tweeds: the modern Harris and also other classy tweeds produced in Scotland, England, Ireland and France. Many of these tweeds were popularised in the 1930s by Coco Chanel. Pastel and glittering tweedy confections are newly fashionable among young women.

Subtle Prince of Wales check on a worsted suiting with performance features

Called Intercity, this fabric by Holland and Sherry reflects current interest in an urban design direction, recasting the classics. Designers are using heritage as a starting point for new ideas. Yarns woven into formal suiting fabrics reflect the greys, blacks and blues of the urban landscape where underlying classic patterns and designs are less easily seen unless you are right next to them. They often have performance features; woven or finished to be non-crease or stain resistant. Urban chic is a major trend in menswear, using traditional fabrics like dark suitings with 3-D effects like birdseyes (small dots).

British clothes with a difference

This is a typical Hackett scenario, at the trendy British brand, where there is often an ironic take on British style and Imperial history. Customers of Hackett, the suave and exciting menswear label, and especially those from USA and all over Europe, appreciate the appeal of top quality fabrics, many of which are sourced from British mills. These mills provide a well-recognised image that is being interpreted by design labels from many countries including blazer stripes and recoloured check designs. In the same way, that other iconic brand Brooks Brothers represents an American Ivy League look each season, where a casual heritage look is interpreted in classic fabrics, high-quality wools, felted surfaces, knitted cardigans, cord trousers and cotton shirts.

A new take on traditional patterns

Fair Isles, snowflake patterns and the characteristic Guernsey designs with special ribbing are newly fashionable. Cables and Arran rope patterns in chunky wool take traditional designs and reinterpret them for a new look that appeals to both men and women. This is a John Smedley design.

**Country meets town modeled
by Ian Bruce**
This suit, by Dashing Tweeds and tailored by
Huntsman Savile Row, is based on traditional tails
but they are 'chopped off'. Heritage designs take the
past and make it totally suited to the present.

A different look for traditional menswear

Ishiro Suzuki is a cutter at Henry Poole, tailors of Savile Row, and a prizewinner in the prestigious Golden Shears competition 2011. This design was for his final Royal College of Art MA show. With its metallic greys and intriguing pattern, Suzuki has a very different take on traditional menswear fabrics.

The barriers between formal and casual wear are breaking down. In chic capitals like Milan, Paris, London and New York traditional suit jackets are being worn with jeans, and casual styling adapted for formal suitings for young people who want less formality. Wool jackets are constructed without a lining to make them light and easy for summer wear. Cerruti, Zegna and Armani are great Italian brands adept at this look

A heritage-inspired theme

Guy Hills, founder of Dashing Tweeds, has made waves in the fashion industry by reviving many different styles and designs, but always with a modern flavour. This is the original Dashing Tweeds suit, fabric designed by Kirsty McDougall, with a Dandy influence, a stylish suit for cycling in. Practicality meets nostalgia with a very modern touch.

Traditional weaving

Traditional weaving skills are still in operation, requiring substantial knowledge from the makers. Bulmer & Lumb in Yorkshire make fabrics from precious fibres to be used by top tailors and major labels.

Flannel on the loom

Heritage qualities and designs like traditional flannels are finding favour with edgy designers. Fox Flannels in the west of England have revived traditional skills of the area, and combine them with directional designs and have achieved great international success.

Traditional Barathea, Covert cloth, speckled Donegals and Prince of Wales checks are the centrepiece of today's designs, recoloured each season by leading mills in Britain and Italy who draw on their archives to recreate them.

21st century kilts by Howie

Proof that Scotsmen in kilts can still strike awe and wonder in the
beholder. Kilts are big business for Scottish textiles. The fabrics
are traditionally woven from wool and many mills can match
most Anglo-Saxon names to a pattern for particular Scottish clans
– very popular for heritage seekers in the US, Canada, Australia,
and even in Japan and China. The tartan kilt has been adopted
for wedding-wear all over the world.

Mini tartan kilt

A new take on tartan cloth, here in bright
colours in a pleated kilt by Scottish
designer Joyce Young, who takes a fresh
look at traditional fabrics. She specialises
in high-quality tartan wedding-wear, often
using conventional wedding dress fabrics
and heritage tartans together.

Childhood Treasures: nostalgic prints by Liberty Art Fabrics (both pages)

Although the Liberty print archive is a treasure house for people who love art, colour and exquisite draughtsmanship, it is also a tangible history of art movements in the 19th and 20th century. Liberty may be associated with pretty flower prints on cotton Tana Lawn. It also has a long tradition of capturing the zeitgeist, commissioning artists to illustrate the spirit of the times with designs from Art Deco to Op Art. The fact that heritage is highly valued puts Liberty at the forefront of contemporary design.

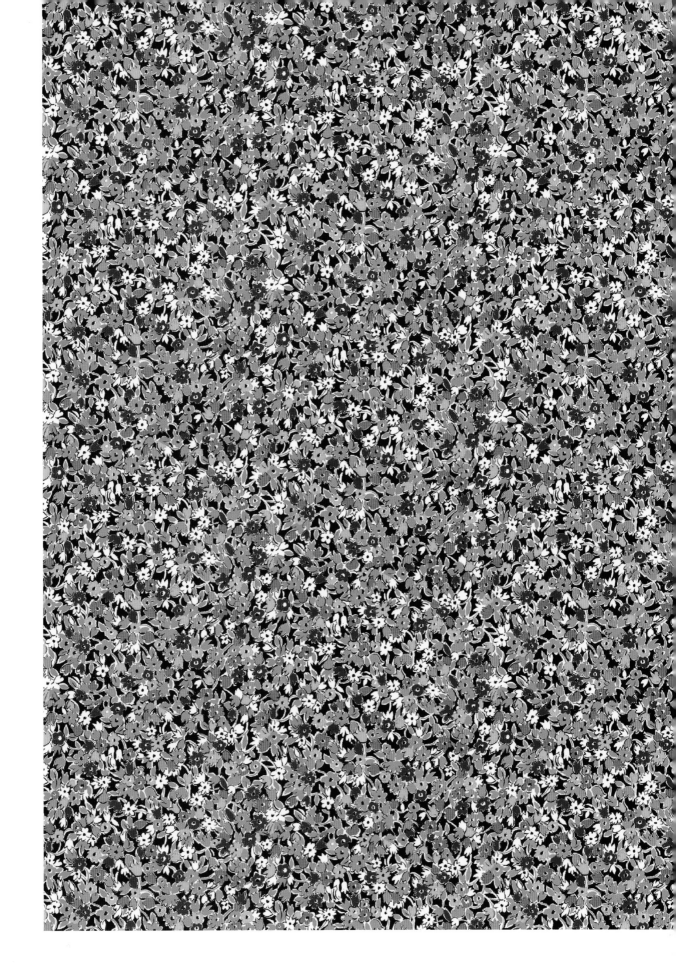

KNITTING

WE ALL wear knits, whether it's chunky cardigans or T-shirts, jersey skirts, jackets, or seamless underwear. Knitted fabrics can be very cheap and cheerful or handmade works of art. Hand knitting is one of the fastest growing areas of fashion, with huge participation by young people, and it is making manufacturers of hand-knitting yarn sit up and take notice.

For knitting, wool is spun and twisted and the piece is constructed by connecting loops using special knitting needles, either a pair of needles or more for circular designs like socks and tubular designs, or using small knitting machines for hand knitting at home. The knotting of complicated designs into the body of the garment is called intarsia and is traditionally done by hand. Crochet involves one hooked needle and connects the wools by twisting and looping into holey patterns for jumpers, skirts and shawls. Lace is usually looped round the hand and small frames.

The same basic techniques apply in knitwear factories, many of the most successful are now located in China, where machines automate knitting at astonishing speed using the latest technology to control speed, colour, design and pattern. Complex jacquard patterns can be programmed into the machines and carried out in minutes while digital printing has transformed the range of effects that can be achieved. It's led to increases in knitted fashion in the shops, with seamless garments, knitted in one, proving important for bodywear, babywear and sportswear. T-shirts and underwear are also knitted. Jersey is one of the great fabrics and can be used for almost any design, including skirts, dresses, gym clothes and jackets.

Knitwear regularly appears on the catwalks in intricate versions by designers from Moschino to Giorgio Armani. Just take a look at the catwalk shows on the Internet from London, New York, Milan and Tokyo each winter season.

At professional yarn fairs Italian companies have been seriously promoting new lightweight blends of wool and silk, expensive mohair and cashmere balls of yarn in directional colours as well as acrylic mixes with texture and colour. Sometimes women with prodigious knitting skills have been recruited to show the buyers what can be done with a pair of knitting needles and the right materials.

The great upsurge in hand knitting of the past few years started slowly, but has gathered pace. You'll notice people knitting on trains and buses on their way to work or while watching tennis matches or waiting in airports. Social networking has provided the impetus for the spread of this revival, which had already started among a generation who had never been taught the skill. Grandmothers have been recruited into schools to pass on their skills and in New York, Paris, Hong Kong, Milan and London knitting cafes have opened up, with groups meeting regularly to share a drink and make new friends over the knitting needles.

There is now a huge international network composed mainly of women, who post pictures of their latest creations for comment. They discuss the merits of different fibres and await the delivery of new batches of yarn in the trending colours that they buy online.

The Internet has also proved a lifeline for small producers of yarn from local breeds of sheep, cashmere goats and alpaca, especially in the US and UK, and some of these

Delicacy of colour in cashmere knitting yarn

This yarn, by Carriagi, will be knitted by machine into high-class garments for designer labels and brands. One of the things which distinguishes high-quality is the attention paid to unusual, sophisticated colour ideas and the transition from one season to the other, with a subtle change of tone. Modern knitting machines are highly automated and can respond to complex instructions, so that garments can have different looks within one garment, tighter in some areas, loose and holey in others, to make layering a fashion option.

producers also spin and dye the yarn themselves. It's also provided them with an outlet for creating their own designs, sometimes going on to sell the finished goods – "the democratisation of fashion", as one producer called it.

Historically, the fishing communities on the islands off Norway, Sweden, or Scotland, or islands such as Fair Isle, Guernsey or Jersey have developed complicated individual patterns for their knitwear made of virtually waterproof, oiled, local sheep's wool. One explanation for these unique local patterns is that they were individually designed to identify bodies of seamen washed up on the shore. Certainly knitting and fishing are interlinked.

These hardwearing jumpers are now sought after all over the world by fashion conscious people looking for style and fascinated by the back-story. The heroine of the cult Danish television series The Killing wears a signature snowflake patterned sweater that has set off a global fashion trend. Sweaters like these are now worn from Moscow to Beijing by smart young people who love the chunky looks of the original chain and rope designs, and the snowflakes and stars.

Young knit designers' dynamic approach, supported by industry in Italy and the UK

RIGHT **Julia Ida Mackenroth**
Julia Ida Mackenroth designed this knitted ensemble with a filmy, delicate looking pastel coloured skirt contrasting with a dark knitted jacket trimmed with the same colour. At the Royal College of Art where she won several awards, Julia had support from Zegna Baruffa Lane Borgosesia, Filpucci and Swarovski.

CENTRE **Lucy Hammond**
An elegant shining tunic in sophisticated colours and a simple shape invested with an air of Eastern opulence by designer Lucy Hammond, also a graduate of the Royal College of Art. Supported by the Worshipful Company of Framework knitters – an ancient Guild in the City of London, Loro Piana, Rowan yarns, and by Swarovski.

FAR RIGHT **Samantha Bushell**
Knitwear is now seen as statement fashion, no longer as merely an accessory. Large windowpane motifs make for a dramatic theme designed by Samantha Bushell at the Royal College of Art. Italian mill support came from Loro Piana, Ecafil Best, Filpucci and Filmar.

Modern bright blue dye used on a thicker yarn, knitted with traditional patterns

Traditional patterns like these chunky, looped stitches with texture and movement are very fashionable. Whether in regular, thicker and coarser wool for authenticity, or in the newer yarns that are lighter in weight, can be washed easily and retain their thickness, jumpers are back in fashion. Winters may be getting colder in some places and with steep rises in the price of fuel, people are looking towards insulating, well-tried solutions like thick wool, worn in layers over finer knits. With offices and homes turning the heating down in cold weather the fashion industry will react in its usual way.

Cosy knit meets cool denim

Knit ideas

Yarn shows and fabric exhibitions are a way for the trade to show off its new inventions and persuade people of the superiority of their developments so that their products might very well appear on the catwalk a season later. But really it's all about colour, fashion, and how the market is feeling. These meetings are a good way of exchanging information. The wonderfully complex stitches shown here were presented to the professionals who were attending, to highlight what could be done with the latest yarns, all worked out by designers Angelo Figus and Nicola Miller.

WEAVING

THE STORY of weaving is as old as that of humanity and is woven into its very existence. The weaving loom was one of the first machines invented. Phrases derived from weaving have entered many languages, especially English. We talk of spinning a yarn, weaving a web of intrigue. Some archaeologists link the intellectual concepts of counting and numbers in early societies with the mechanics of counting threads and working out the mathematics and geometry of the warp and the weft in weaving.

Because fabric biodegrades and disappears over time, it is a mystery exactly when and where the art of weaving first developed, but traces of such activity have been found dating back to prehistoric times. There are some indications that weaving was already known in the Palaeolithic era. Neolithic textiles have been traced back to 5000 years BCE. The earliest evidence of textiles for clothing comes from tiny fascinating scraps of woven fabric found in graves in the Middle East and central Europe.

Weaving developed across different cultures and civilisations over thousands of years. The long heritage of spinning and weaving has inserted itself into history, politics and tradition. Money from the wool trade and the development of banking founded the di Medici fortunes and stimulated the Renaissance in Italy 600 years ago. The growing demand for textiles and advances in machinery were a factor in driving the Industrial Revolution in England in the late 18th to early 19th century.

Today in the textile trade the appreciation of heritage has led to designers and buyers trawling through the archives of once great mills all over Europe, looking through the pattern books and finding inspiration for modern interpretations. US designers started the trend decades ago, and the significance of the archive has been recognised by many of the very successful surviving enterprises which have recognised that their past is also their future.

Ethnic patterns and traditions are cherished as inspiration for new generations: African prints, Indian weaves, Indonesian dyeing techniques and patterns. Another source for patterns and weaves from the past are secondhand and vintage shops.

Harris Tweed is an iconic heritage fabric; woven on the Island of Harris from Scottish wool, it is hand loomed by crofters and lasts forever. Only fabrics made in this way and in the Outer Hebrides can be labelled Harris Tweed. Every piece bears the orb mark that identifies it as the genuine article. The cloth is sold all over the world. It has been used on trendy sneakers and baseball shoes for today's fashion followers, and to recreate the past in countless films and television shows, including the signature jacket of Dr Who. It lives in the past and the present.

Traditional skills of weaving

These images show stages that are part of the traditional skills of weaving showing the dyed wool fibre ready to be processed, carded, and made ready for spinning.

*Yarn on the loom
ready to be woven*
Begg creates high-quality
scarves and stoles and
cashmere accessories that
are seen on the catwalks
of the world.

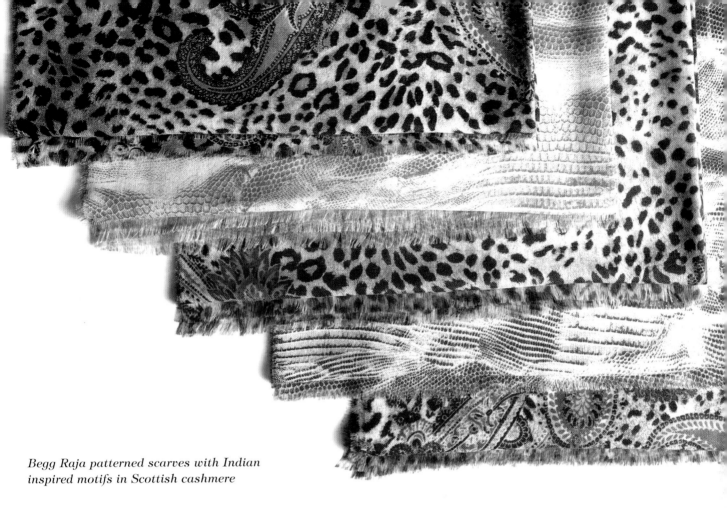

*Begg Raja patterned scarves with Indian
inspired motifs in Scottish cashmere*

*A luminously beautiful
piece of Harris Tweed
on a hand loom, with
its shuttle*

The traditional clan Thomson tartan

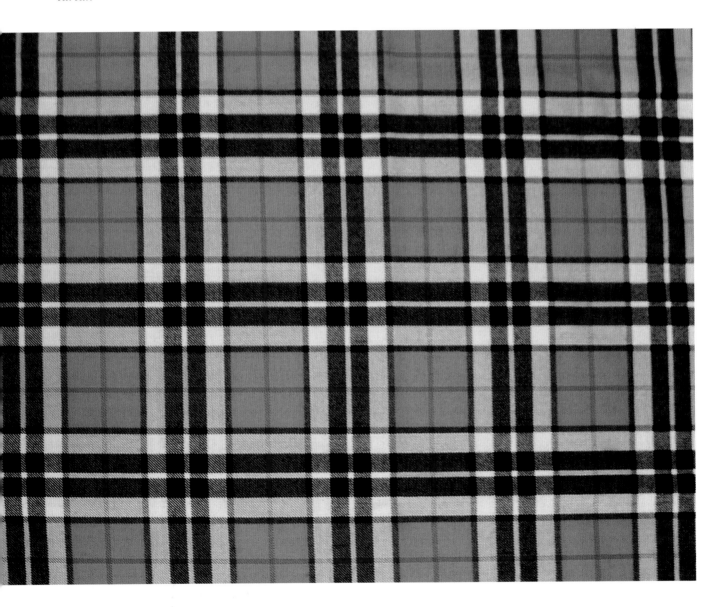

Traditional wool tartan

This traditional tartan is shown on
a modern loom-wide width and
computerised processes allow it to be
woven at great speed. This tartan and the
one opposite were woven at Lochcarron.

Skilled craftsmanship

A skilled worker at Fox Brothers carrying out traditional weaving
and mending skills on modern heritage inspired designs

Sophisticated weaves

Subtle colour variations which can be achieved by sophisticated
design, several of which have very descriptive names, like this
Sharkskin Supreme. This suiting is fine worsted wool by Holland
and Sherry.

6

Fabric to fashion

Fabric to fashion

DESIGNERS spend more time on selecting the right fabrics than on any other stage of making fashion. Having looked at the wide range of fabrics available and their attributes in the previous chapters, the statement that 'fashion starts with fabric' should be understandable.

Few people outside the trade are conscious that every season thousands of international buyers, designers, manufacturers, spinners, knitters, weavers and the world's press move around the world to fabric exhibitions as well as cultural events, gathering information, getting ready to play their part in an elaborate game of prediction.

Textiles involve commodity trading, industrial investment and artistic flair. Mills have to buy the fibres on global markets, spin the yarns, select the colours for the season's dyes, weave or knit the fabrics, produce the prints and patterns ready for the designers who will create their signature creations for a new season. It's big business with a long lead-time. And it has a lot of influence on how we live.

The textile trade links almost every country, from people herding animals in remote nomadic communities to large-scale crop growing, all providing the fibres that will be woven into textiles. The textiles business involves investment in chemicals and plant on an industrial scale, and it includes small groups of urban people going off to raise animals in the countryside and making things by hand. It gives rise to amazing artistic expression, created by designers driven by a vision and by people with complex specialist skills handed down through generations.

The eco movement started with textiles, influencing the industry from top to bottom. The textiles trade took the lead in reducing carbon emissions, investigating ecologically and socially sound production and responding to current concerns. The best companies have radically reworked their manufacturing processes to introduce sustainability into a technical industry that is also intimately connected to the land, farming and local economies--a circle sometimes difficult to square.

It may seem counterintuitive to say, but when money is short, customers tend to buy better quality. We want to make sure that our money is spent wisely on fashion which will last

RIGHT *Fashion drama*
Flowing, silky fabric and peacock colours in relaxed luxury style from Rajinder Johal, a graduate from the Royal College of Art. The accessories are by RCA fellow graduates.

OPPOSITE Vivienne Westwood gives a make-over to Australian Merino wool for her Gold collection.

better and which is fun and comfortable to wear. There is also a marked move by professionals to choose higher quality and the choice of fabric is key. The idea of heritage and tradition appeals to a whole new generation who are worried about the environment and about society's throwaway habits, and this also supports the idea of quality over quantity.

The fabric world has its own momentum and even its own arcane signs. The mark of someone who works in textiles is the irresistible urge they have to feel the fabric worn by the person they are with, rubbing it between finger and thumb during the course of a conversation--something which is quite disconcerting to those new to the trade, but vital in finding out how good the fabric is. In fact, it's quite a good rule of thumb for everyone, together with looking at the fibre content on the label hidden in your clothes, pick up the fabric and feel it.

Don't hesitate to seek more knowledge about the fabrics you choose. The better garment-makers will respond with information, making it easier to make an informed choice. Of course it's the designers who work their magic on the textiles we've talked about, turning it into fashion, but it's good to know what you're wearing. So always read the label!

Long, flimsy and delicate retro cotton dress with Indian print, designed by Milly NY, known for vintage chic.

Eley Kishimoto, the ultra cool London fashion duo, famous for their elegant quirky fabric designs, here printed on paper columns for an exhibition.

*Embroidery brings out the swirling African motif
on this sky blue cotton from Lagos Fashion Week*

Fading into nothingness

Finely knitted dress shows delicacy and contrast at Feel the Yarn annual competition 2012, where selected young designers from colleges around the world can work with the very latest luxury yarns. This design is by Hannah Jenkinson of New York's Parsons, The New School for Design.

French fashion house Carven show at Pitti Immagine Uomo
Groups of 'waiters' raced around a track with laden trays, with bicycling models wearing the designs, while the fashion crowd feasted on formal tables on a sports pitch. It's tough work, sometimes, being a fashion journalist.

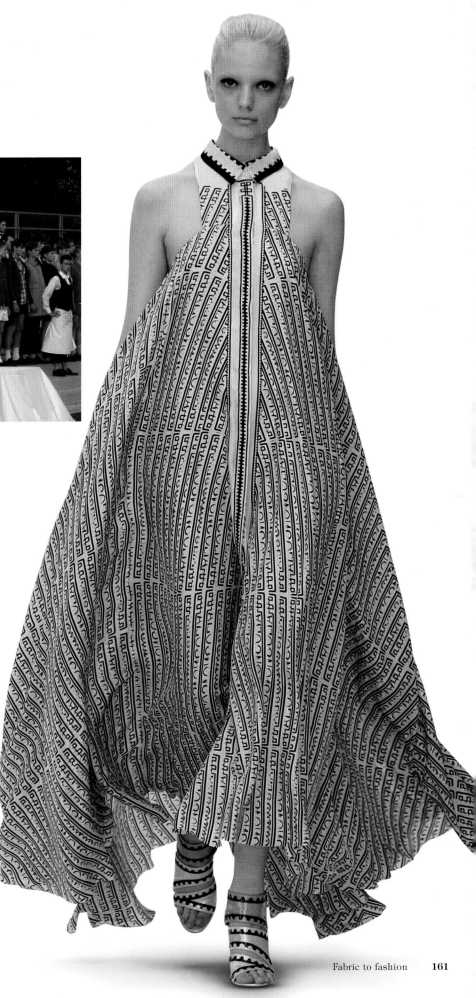

A flowing digital print from Mary Katrantzou shown for spring/summer 2013

There is nothing 'little' about this black dress in pleated silk
This dress by Giles Deacon was on show at the recent Ballgowns exhibition at the Victoria & Albert Museum.

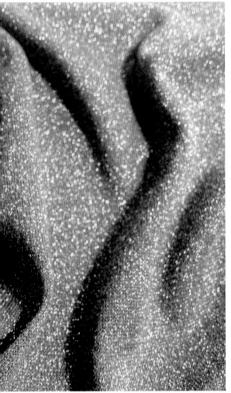

**How to get the essential classy
sophisticated sparkle**
Highly technical Lurex yarn is embedded
in this wool knit by Italian spinner Zegna
Baruffa.

Contrasting textures
Silk, transparency and metallic
ornament can be seen in this
multi-fabric creation by Rodarte,
spring/summer 2013 collection.

The power of pattern
Ethnic inspired pattern in bold colours. Polyester dress, made in Italy, from James Lakeland, England.

Light and airy pastel mohair knit by African Expressions, in a design called Love, made from Cape Mohair

Chunky knitted coat shown in lightweight wool with faux fur collar at Italian spinner Di Ve

The internationally popular British look with its iconic heritage factors, and British patterns and fabrics, here by Smart Turnout

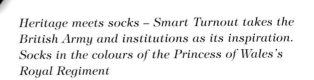

Heritage meets socks – Smart Turnout takes the British Army and institutions as its inspiration. Socks in the colours of the Princess of Wales's Royal Regiment

Shining silk from Italy's age-old heritage area of silk expertise. Como, still the centre of excellence

Fabric as art
Inventive ideas in Pitti Filati research area, painted knits,
shining colours, mixed media and a Renaissance feel.
Designed by Figus and Miller.

Flashy outfit by Lou de Testa, winner of Podium Jeunes Stylistes, France, with mix of coated fabrics and finishes to make a statement

ABOVE *Yarns by Zegna Baruffa, be-mi-va and Miroglio in linen, cotton and rayon viscose explored by Figus and Miller in Pitti Filati, attracting buyers and stylists*

RIGHT *Colette Vermeulen, from the Royal College of Art, with a smart young fashion look with confident styling and clever use of colour and texture*

LEFT *Funky looks and high quality tailoring fabrics united by Femme de Rose, London*

Unmistakably Chanel
FAR LEFT Coral fabric is decorated
with pearls. Colours reflect
a sea-change.
CENTRE Using ice cream
colours, a Coco-inspired
Chanel jacket in contrast trim
light tweed over frothy pink
skirt.
LEFT Lagerfeld uses minimalist
detailing and intricate shaping
on a pearly white creation for
Chanel.

Picture credits

Every effort has been made to credit the appropriate source, but if you find any omissions or errors please contact us. We will undertake to make any corrections in the next printing.

Courtesy Sudwolle, Germany, pp 10–11; courtesy Hainsworth, UK, p 12; courtesy of the Woolmark Company, pp 13, 16 (left), 17 (bottom), 157; courtesy of Loro Piana, Italy p 14; courtesy British Wool Marketing Board, p 15; courtesy of The New Zealand Merino Company, p 16 (right); courtesy Lochcarron of Scotland, p 17 (top), 150–151; courtesy Escorial group.com, p 18 (top); courtesy Scabal, Belgium, pp 18, 20; courtesy of Crombie.co.uk, p 20 (bottom); courtesy Filpucci, Italy/photo: Tilde de Tullio, pp 21, 86 (right); courtesy Successori Reda, Italy, p 22; courtesy Lanificio Angelico, Italy p 23 (top); courtesy Dormeuil, p 23 (bottom); courtesy Texprint, pp 24–25, 55 (top); courtesy Alfred Brown, UK, p26 (top); courtesy of John Smedley, UK pp 26 (top), 27, 131; courtesy Alan Paine, UK, p 28 (top); courtesy of Timothy Everest, pp 28 (bottom), 29; courtesy of John Foster, pp 30, 48, 49; courtesy Textiles Scotland, pp 32, 33 (bottom), 136 (right), 141, 146–147, 149; courtesy Todd & Duncan, Scotland, pp 34–35, 126 (bottom); courtesy Cariaggi, Italy, pp 36, 37 (top), 120, 140; courtesy Johnstons of Elgin/photo © Angus Bremner, p 37 (bottom); courtesy Pitti Immagine/photo: JR Prescott, p 38, 86 (left), 168; courtesy Flagstaff Alpacas, Dunedin, NZ, p 39 (top), 40 (bottom); courtesy Michells/photo: JR Prescott, p39 (bottom); courtesy Pure English Alpaca, p 40 (top); courtesy Douglas Creek, NZ, p 42 (top), 43; courtesy De Pio, Italy, p 42 (bottom); courtesy Mohair South Africa, p 44; courtesy Cape Mohair Spinners, p 45 (top); courtesy African Expressions, SA, p 45 (bottom); courtesy Samuel Tweed, UK, pp 46–47; courtesy of Richard Weston, pp 50–51; courtesy Pitti Immagine W/photo: JR Prescott, p 52 (left), 85, 86 (left), 159; Photo by Oli Scarff/Getty Images, p 53; courtesy of Botto Poala, Italy/photo: JR Prescott, p 54; courtesy of MyaBlue Luxe.co.uk, p 55 (bottom); courtesy Pitti Immagine Uomo/ photo: JR Prescott, pp 56–57, 61, 78, 145 (top); courtesy Liberty Art Fabrics, pp 58–59, 72–73, 138–139; courtesy Mark Thomas Taylor, UK, pp 60, 66, 69 (bottom); courtesy Albini Group, Italy, pp 62–64; courtesy of Denim by PV, Paris, pp 67, 68, 69 (top); The Cotton Bride: Courtesy Cotton Incorporated, p 70 (left); courtesy MYB Textiles, p 70 (right); courtesy Textiles Scotland/photo: Adrian Lourie, p 71 (top); Monique L'huillier design: Courtesy Cotton Incorporated, p 71 (bottom); courtesy CELC/Masters of Linen, pp 74, 75 (middle & bottom), 77, 79, 81, 83 (bottom), 110 (right); courtesy Solbiati, Italy, pp 82–83 (top); © The acclaimed Rocca Fantasia by Andy Warhol for the 1983 Filpucci advertising campaign, p 84; courtesy Filpucci, Italy/Pitti Immagine Filati, p 85; courtesy Outsider Design/ pictures by Jeffrey Boudreau, pp 88, 89 (top); courtesy Lenzing, p 89 (bottom); courtesy Schoeller, Switzerland, pp 90–91, 100–101, 118; courtesy Stone Island/Pitti Immagine Uomo/photo: JR Prescott, p 99; courtesy Hot Squash, UK, p 102 (left); courtesy Coolmax®, p 102 (right); courtesy Eschler/Arc'teryx, Canada, p 103; courtesy Dashing Tweeds UK, pp 104, 132, 133 (right); courtesy CuteCircuit, p 105; courtesy Rapanui Clothing, UK, pp 109, 114; courtesy Filatura Miroglio, Italy/courtesy CLASS, p 111; courtesy Miroglio, Italy, pp 112–113 (bottom); courtesy Outsider Design/photo: Steven Aron Williams, p 115 (top); courtesy Outsider Design/photo: Andrew Edgecumbe, p 115 (bottom); courtesy NEWLIFE® by Filatura Miroglio at CLASS, pp 116, 117; Buhler yarn/courtesy Oeko-Tex, p 119; courtesy Marks & Spencer, p 121; courtesy Feel the Yarn, Italy, pp 122–123; courtesy Harris Tweed Hebrides/photo: Pierre Guillemin, pp 126 (top), 128; courtesy Holland & Sherry, p 129, 153; courtesy Hackett, p 130; courtesy Bulmer & Lumb, p 134; courtesy Fox Brothers & Co, UK, pp 135, 152; courtesy Howie/picture by Alban Donohoe, p 136 (left); courtesy Cariaggi, Italy, p 140; courtesy Royal College of Art, pp 142, 156, 171 (middle); courtesy Pitti Immagine Filati, p 145 (bottom), 168, 171 (top); courtesy Begg Scotland, pp 148, 149 (left); Francois Guillot/AFP/Getty Images p 154–155; courtesy Eley Kishimoto, p 158 (bottom); Milly NY/courtesy Cotton Incorporated, p 158 (right); courtesy Feel the Yarn, p 160; courtesy Pitti Immagine Uomo/Carven Show, p 161 (top); photo by Antonio de Moraes Barros Filho/WireImage, p 161 (bottom); photo by Chiaki Nozu/WireImage p 162 (left); courtesy Zegna Baruffa/photo: JR Prescott, p 163 (left); Victor Virgile/Gamma-Rapho via Getty Images, p 163 (right); courtesy www.jameslakeland.net, p 164; courtesy African Expressions, SA, p 165 (top); courtesy Como Silk/photo: JR Prescott, p 167; courtesy Podium Jeunes Stylistes, France, p 169; courtesy Femme de Rose, London, p 170; courtesy Chanel Press Office, p 173.

Acknowledgements

Special thanks to:

The Woolmark Company/AWI
Masters of Linen/CELC
Cotton Incorporated
Schoeller Textiles
Cape Mohair Spinners, South Africa
New Zealand Merino
Cervelt
British textiles: luxury knitters and weavers, especially those Yorkshire mills who took special pictures
Textiles Scotland
Harris Tweed

The Royal College of Art and MA graduates for demonstrating what exceptional talent and expertise can do with textiles
Texprint's young designers for marvellous examples of fabric creativity and fashion industry support.
Teacake Tuesday for expertise on the green agenda
The continuous support received from the Italian textile industry;
Many Italian luxury brands, spinners and weavers
Pitti Immagine, who have generously invited me to Florence so many times,
The hospitality of Milano Unica and Filo.
Premiere Vision Paris
and Chanel for glimpses of high fashion

INDEX

A

Acne Studios 110
African Expressions 45, 46–7, 48–9, 165
Alan Paine 28
Alexander Begg Cashmere 37, 148–9
Alfred Brown (Worsted Mills) Ltd 26
alpaca 38–40
Angora goats 44–5
animal welfare 114
anti-bacterial fabric 21, 44, 84, 85, 98, 108
archives, textile 146
Arc'teryx 103
Armani, Giorgio 38, 94, 116, 119, 133, 140
Australia 13–15, 18, 19, 114

B

bamboo 84, 110, 114
Barathea 134
bast fibres 74
black fabrics 98
bluesign® standard 118
bottles, plastic (recycled) 113, 119
British Isles 15, 44, 45, 130, 134–5
Bulmer & Lumb 134
Bushell, Samantha 142–3

C

c_change™ technology 94
camel hair 38
Campaign for Wool 15, 31
Cariaggi 36, 37, 120
cashmere 32–7, 66, 86, 120, 126, 134, 140, 148–9
cervelt 42–3
Chanel 172–3
checks 15, 28–9, 62–3, 82, 129, 134
chemicals 60, 108, 114, 120
Cheviot cloth 15
chiffon 77
childrenswear 40, 81
China 23, 33, 45, 50, 96, 108, 114, 119, 140
Chitosan 89
coats 38, 74, 79
Coldblack® 98
colours 23, 32–7, 40, 69, 80, 96, 116, 129, 144
Coolmax® 94, 102
corn fibre 86
cosmetic fabrics 98
cotton 61–73, 94, 110, 158
   organic and sustainable 62, 114–15
   recycled 113, 119
Covert cloth 134
crab shells (Crabyon®) 84, 89
cria 40
crochet 140

Crombie, the 20
CuteCircuit 105
cycling clothes 94, 96–7, 102, 133

D

Dashing Tweeds 104, 132, 133
denim 62, 66–9
designers 156, 158
young 24, 49, 122–3, 142–3, 160, 169
diamonds 29, 96
digital printing 50, 77, 105, 126, 140
Donegal tweeds and knits 15, 134
Dormeuil 21, 23
dyeing techniques 77, 146
dyes, natural 36, 110, 112, 120

E

easy-care fabrics 15, 17, 61, 63, 74
ecological fabrics and issues 60, 106–23, 156, 158
   alpaca 40
   cotton 62, 114–15
   Ingeo™ 86
   linen 74, 76, 78, 80, 110
   natural dyes 36, 110, 112, 120
   unusual materials 86
   viscose 84, 87, 88
   wool 15, 118
Egypt 61, 63, 64, 74
elastane 96
electronic fabrics 105
emissions 108, 112, 118, 156
Eschler 96
Escorial sheep 15, 18
ethnic patterns 146, 149, 158–9, 164
Everest, Timothy 28
expertise 66

F

Fair Isles 15, 131, 142
Feel the Yarn 122–3, 160
Figus, Angelo 145, 168, 171
Filpucci 21, 84
finishing 30, 61–2, 74, 79, 94, 98, 101
fish skins 86
fishing communities 142
flannels 134–5
flax 74, 75, 77, 80
Fox Brothers & Co 134–5, 152

G

genetic modification (GM) 60, 62
Global Organic Textile Standards (GOTS) 108
golf wear 102–3
Gore-tex® 94, 95
Guernsey 15, 131, 142

H

H&M 120
Hackett 130
Hainsworth, A W 12
Hammond, Lucy 142–3
handmade textiles 108
Harris tweed 15, 126, 128, 146, 149
health-monitoring fabrics 105
Henry Poole & Co 12, 133
heritage fabrics 124–53, 158, 166–7
'hot pants' (heated fabric) 96

I

Ichiro Suzuki 133
Ingeo™ 86
intarsia 140
Internet 114, 140
Italy 22, 60, 61, 80, 113, 140, 146, 167
   cashmere 32, 36, 37

J

jackets 76, 78, 104
jeans 62, 66–9
Jersey 15, 142
jersey (fabric) 140
Jockey 64
John Foster 30, 48, 49
John Smedley 26, 27, 131
Johnstons of Elgin 37

K

Kenzo 80–1
Kevlar 98–9
Khamisani, Noorin 88, 114
kilts 136–7
knitting 140–5
knitwear 26–8, 55, 85, 140–5
   alpaca 38, 40
   cashmere 32–7
   designer 142–3, 160, 163, 165, 168
   lightweight 17, 26
   linen 74, 82, 110
   mohair 44–9
   patterns 26, 131, 140, 142

L

labels 26
lace 70–1, 140
layering 94, 103
Lenpur 84
Lenzing 84, 89
Li Xiao 122–3
Libeco 79, 80
Liberty prints 72–3, 138–9
linen 74–83, 94, 110
'London Shrunk' finish 30
looms 71, 135, 147, 148–9, 151

Loro Piana 14, 94
Lurex 32, 86, 163
luxury fabrics 23, 30, 41, 42, 47, 52, 62, 63
Lycra® 101

M
McCartney, Stella 80
Mackay, Donald John 128
Mackenroth, Julia Ida 142
Marks & Spencer 108, 120–1
Masters of Linen 77
memory 100–1
Merino sheep 13, 15, 16, 19, 28, 98, 142,
    156–7
metallic yarns and fabrics 21, 98
microclimate technology 94, 95, 103
Miller, Nicola 145, 168, 171
Miroglio 113, 116, 117, 119, 171
Modal 84
mohair 44–9, 165
moisture management 19, 55, 61, 62, 65,
    84, 89, 94, 102, 103
MYB Textiles 70, 71

N
nanotechnology 94, 98
Naturetec 118
New Zealand 15, 16, 18, 38, 39, 40, 42,
    44, 114
NewLife® 113, 116, 119
nylon 94, 118

O
Oeko-Tex® 108, 119
organic fabrics 28, 40, 52, 62, 78, 87, 108,
    114–15
outdoor clothing 26, 48, 74, 79, 94, 103,
    118
Outlast® 94
Outsider 88, 114–15

P
Phase Change Materials (PCMs) 94
Pitti Immagine Filati 38, 85, 86, 145, 168,
    171
Pitti Immagine Uomo 56–7, 61, 78, 145,
    161
polyamide 79, 93, 94, 98
polyester 92, 93, 94, 96, 101, 102, 113,
    164
    recycled 117, 119
Prato, Italy 113
precious stones 20, 21, 96
Pret pour Partir 79
protective clothing 92, 93, 96, 98, 105
provenance 16

R
ramie 74
Rapanui Clothing 87, 109, 114
rayon 84

recycling 108, 109, 111, 113, 117, 118,
    119, 120, 122
reflective yarns 104
research 96
Royal College of Art 122, 133, 142, 156,
    171

S
Safilin 82
Savile Row 12, 15, 18, 28, 31, 41, 76,
    132–3
Saxonies 18
Scabal 18, 20
Schoeller 94, 98, 101, 118
Scotland 15, 32–3, 37, 71, 126–7, 128
    tartans 15, 17, 28, 136–7, 150–1
seashells 84, 89
second-hand clothing 109, 126, 146
self-cleaning fabric 98
selvedge, woven 14
shirts and shirting 61, 62–3, 69, 111
shoes 83, 94, 128, 146
shows 22, 24, 66, 86, 122, 140, 145, 156
silk 50–7, 110, 163, 167
silver 21, 98, 108
skiwear 94, 96
Slow Fashion 60, 108, 113
smart textiles 105
socks 42, 98, 166
Solbiati 82
South Africa 13, 44, 45
spider's silk 50–2, 53
sportswear 15, 92, 94, 95, 101, 102–3, 108,
    118, 140
Stone Island 98
suiting 129, 152–3
suits 18, 20, 28–30, 38, 41, 104, 105, 132–3
    linen 78, 81
    mohair 44, 48, 49
sustainability 62, 108, 118–23, 156

T
Taiana 111, 117
tartans 15, 17, 28, 136–7, 150–1
Teflon 17, 79, 98
Tencel 84, 89
Texprint 24, 55
thermo-regulating fabrics 94, 96, 98, 103
Tintoria di Quaregna 110, 112
Todd & Duncan 33, 126
Toogood, Harriet 24–5
traceability 120
trade, textile 146, 156
tweeds 15, 104, 126, 128, 146, 149

U
underwear 65, 84
uniforms 12
upcycling 119
urban chic 129
UV protection 15, 17, 96, 98

V
vicuña 41
vintage clothing 44, 45, 109, 116
viscose 84–9

W
Warhol, Andy 84
weaving 44, 60, 134–5, 146–53
Weston, Richard 50–1
Westwood, Vivienne 15, 16, 128, 142,
    156–7
wicking treatments 61–2, 65, 94, 95
wood pulp 84
wool 12–31, 33, 66, 133, 140–5, 146
    blends 12, 32, 38, 41, 48, 49, 54, 55, 79
    climate-control qualities 94, 98
    ecological credentials 15, 118
    finishing 30, 98
    machine-washable 15, 17, 118
    recycled 113, 119
    stain-resistant 17, 98
Woolmark 15, 144
worsted system 15, 18, 23, 129, 152–3

Y
Ying Wu 55
Yorkshire mills 12, 18, 23, 26, 38, 44, 45,
    47, 112
Young, Joyce 136–7

Z
Zegna, Ermenegildo 94, 98, 133
Zegna Baruffa Lane Borgosesia 163, 171
zippers 96